T0220275

TECHNOLOGY
MADE SIMPLE FOR
THE TECHNICAL
RECRUITER,
SECOND EDITION

TECHNOLOGY
MADE SIMPLE FOR THE TECHNICAL RECRUITER,
SECOND EDITION

A TECHNICAL SKILLS PRIMER

OBI OGBANUFE

TECHNOLOGY MADE SIMPLE FOR THE TECHNICAL RECRUITER, SECOND EDITION
A TECHNICAL SKILLS PRIMER

iUniverse books may be ordered through booksellers or by contacting:

iUniverse
1663 Liberty Drive
Bloomington, IN 47403
www.iuniverse.com
1-800-Authors (1-800-288-4677)

Because of the dynamic nature of the Internet, any web addresses or links contained in this book may have changed since publication and may no longer be valid. The views expressed in this work are solely those of the author and do not necessarily reflect the views of the publisher, and the publisher hereby disclaims any responsibility for them.

Any people depicted in stock imagery provided by Getty Images are models, and such images are being used for illustrative purposes only. Certain stock imagery © Getty Images.

ISBN: 978-1-5320-6499-9 (sc)
ISBN: 978-1-5320-6498-2 (e)

Library of Congress Control Number: 2019900200

Print information available on the last page.

iUniverse rev. date: 04/24/2019

CONTENTS

For Chris, Chinedu, and Uzo

PREFACE

The technical recruiter is an individual whose job it is to *search for*, *validate*, and *present* qualified candidates to an organization. Such candidates must meet both the technical and nontechnical requirements of the roles they would fill. The understanding of the organization's requirements is the key to searching within the right pool of candidates. The ability to validate that candidates' technical skills match the organization's requirements varies based on the expertise of each technical recruiter. This book outlines the skills technical recruiters need in order to search for, validate, and present good qualified technical candidates to their hiring organizations.

Given that the typical technical recruiter is in constant contact with technical candidates and trying to match their skills and experiences with a hiring organization's requirements, it is important that the recruiter understands the technologies and processes used by both the candidate and hiring organization. In this book, the technical recruiter learns how and why these technologies are used. The technical recruiter also learns questions to ask to ascertain the skills and experience of the candidates and to understand the hiring organization's technology environment.

About the Second Edition

Since the publication of the first edition of this book, I have received questions asking when the second edition would come out. Well ...

it took eight years to get here. A lot has happened in the technology space in the meantime, and I have addressed some of the changes in this edition.

I have added three new chapters, namely "Information Security," "Big Data," and "Cloud Computing." When the first edition was published in 2010, these topics were not as pervasive and widely discussed as they are today. Information security has always been an issue in information systems, but it started to garner increased attention as more and more high-profile organizations became victims of security breaches. Today, information security is ranked as one of the top three issues facing organizations.

The use of big data and cloud computing technologies has grown over the past eight years. In discussing cloud computing, I also highlight the corresponding growth of DevOps processes.

In turn, these focus areas bring with them new and updated sets of tools, technologies, and processes. As a technical recruiter, a key to finding the right candidates to manage such new and updated tools and processes is an understanding of the technologies and their related job roles. A firm understanding of these will help you understand the organization's requirements as well as identify potential candidates to handle these aspects that are so important to an organization's growth and sustainability.

What You Will Find in This Book

In this edition, you will also discover updated and essential skills a technical recruiter must develop in the world of technical recruitment. The primary challenge faced by technical recruiters is this: to understand technology in order to grasp the technical needs of the hiring companies and validate the candidates' skills against the position requirements.

Recruiting is a consulting job and as such, demands that technical recruiters learn and understand the problems their clients face.

For example, when filling a software project manager position, a recruiter should know why a project manager with ten years of experience and project management certification (PMP) may not be suitable for a company that requires a project manager for their software development projects. Could it be that what they really need is a technical project manager? As the recruiting consultant, are you able to ask the kinds of questions that would reveal the real need?

Whether you are new to technical recruiting or an experienced recruiter, this book will guide you as you continue to learn more about this increasingly evolving field. No longer will you be intimidated by the technology acronyms and initialisms in résumés and job descriptions. You will be able to ask pointed and direct questions to understand your client's needs and to validate a candidate's technical capabilities. You will learn why certifications are required by your hiring managers, the type of technologies employed in the hiring organizations, and which requirements are core to a given position.

Who Should Read This Book

Although the primary audience for this book is technical recruiters, it is also for anyone interested in becoming familiar with skill sets in the field of technology. A person seeking to change careers and transition into the technology arena will find this book useful for learning what the requirements are for specific technical roles.

For technical recruiters, whether corporate or contract, new or experienced, this book is an essential technical skills handbook that outlines the basics of technology and its foundations; categorizes the skills required for certain jobs, including application development, software testing, DevOps, and software engineering; and highlights the differences between database administration, database engineering, and other jobs.

This book will help the technical recruiter talk the talk with candidates and hiring managers with confidence. This confidence will benefit not only the experienced recruiter but also newer recruiters who desire to continuously update their knowledge of the tools of their trade.

The corporate recruiter reading this book will deepen his or her knowledge of the technical jargon and makeup of job roles specific to his or her current workplace. This understanding will help in creating new job role descriptions to attract desired candidates and also to help in implementing first-round interviews to qualify candidates.

Hiring managers looking to complement their current arsenal of technical skills will find this book very useful when interviewing external technical recruiters for the purpose of ensuring the recruiter has the necessary technical knowledge to recruit the right candidates.

Human resources departments can use this book as a complementary resource guide for selecting internal technical recruiters.

Lastly, this book is also for individuals who are neither recruiters nor hiring managers but who are interested in understanding the job roles in the technology realm as a whole.

Where to Start

You can easily jump into this book at any point from beginning to end. It has been written in such a way that a reader can start from any chapter and flip through to find sample job descriptions and résumé highlights of a given job role. There are also sample conversations between recruiter and candidate sprinkled throughout the book.

Each chapter ends with a "What We Learned" section, which is a bulleted list of nuggets of information that serve as reminders of the key concepts of that chapter.

How This Book Is Structured

In this edition, you will find thirteen chapters, each broken down into four sections. You will find the terms *client* and *hiring manager* used interchangeably in the course of this book, as their meaning is the same, the hiring manager being the client of the recruiter.

Section 1 (Chapters 1–3)

The *technical job requisition* is introduced in chapter 1 as one of the initial documents a technical recruiter encounters. The job requisition is analyzed to find possible questions for the hiring manager. Unless you have recruited the same job description for the same client for several years, you cannot always assume you know what the hiring manager wants in a candidate. Chapter 1 analyzes a real-world job description to find answers to questions that might have otherwise been assumed or remained hidden, thus leading to a failed recruiting process.

Chapter 2 discusses the *technical résumé*. Although recruiters scan through a vast number of résumés on a day-to-day basis, it's still important to identify and analyze the selected ones for answers—answers to questions identified from the job requisition. This chapter also looks at the link between the résumé and job description, how to identify and avoid skill embellishment, and how to identify and ask questions derived from a résumé.

Chapter 3 looks at the *technology team* and its makeup. The organizational chart is introduced to identify decision makers at client organizations. This chapter also identifies and reviews the role descriptions of key players in a technology company. The chief information security officer and DevOps are introduced in this chapter.

Section 2 (Chapters 4–5)

Chapter 4 discusses *fundamentals of networking* as the foundation for technology as we know it today. In this chapter, readers will benefit from information about network layers, types of networks, the advantages of one over the other, as well as network protocols and how they interact.

Chapter 5 deals with *operating system fundamentals*. It describes the difference between operating systems, especially server operating systems versus desktop operating systems. In this chapter, the reader is also introduced to the skill set requirements for major operating systems like UNIX, Windows, and Mainframe. This chapter also describes the difference between the administrator, engineer, and architect roles.

Section 3 (Chapters 6–8)

Chapter 6 looks at the *software development life cycle (SDLC)*, the makeup and process of the SDLC, how they affect the development process, as well as what job descriptions (positions) fit into each phase of the process and how they interact. This chapter also reviews a real-life development process and the part that the SDLC plays in it.

Chapter 7 covers *software development technologies* and describes the types of programming languages. This chapter also reviews software categories, including web applications, desktop applications, mobile applications, and systems development. Development architecture, methodologies, and frameworks are also highlighted in this chapter. Tables are included that illustrate and classify development technologies specific to each tiered architecture.

Chapter 8 deals with *software testing* and how it differs from quality assurance. The role of software testers and their skill requirements are discussed. This chapter also examines the typical job description of a software tester and some sample recruiter questions.

Section 4 (Chapters 9–13)

Chapter 9 discusses *database technologies* found in business intelligence, data reporting, database development, administration, data warehousing, and data mining. This chapter also describes four major database job roles and includes some sample recruiter questions for each of them. In addition, a summary table that contrasts each role against the others is provided.

Chapter 10 covers *big data*, differentiating it from traditional database systems and reviewing why it is important today. Technologies and applications related to big data are discussed, specifically the Hadoop ecosystem and other technologies used by specialists in this area. This chapter also delves into the typical job description of a big data analyst and some sample recruiter questions.

Chapter 11 examines *information security* and provides an overview and the goals of information security. Examples of threats, vulnerabilities, and attacks are provided. In addition, the chief information security officer (CISO) organization and specific job roles in that organization are explored. The job description of an information security engineer is discussed along with some sample recruiter questions.

Chapter 12 provides an overview of and discusses *cloud computing*, specifically exploring why organizations migrate to the cloud. This chapter discusses cloud computing technologies and processes that recruiters will encounter in job descriptions and résumés. It further describes DevOps and its place in cloud computing jobs. The job description of a cloud engineer is discussed along with some sample recruiter questions.

Chapter 13 explores *certifications* and examines why they are still valuable. This chapter answers various questions about certifications and why organizations need certified candidates. Certifications in information security, software development, database management, project management, operating systems, and networking are discussed.

Now, come walk with me as you familiarize yourself with the technology you talk about every day and, in so doing, gain confidence and enhance your competence for evaluating technical candidates and communicating with hiring managers.

ICONS USED IN THIS BOOK

This book includes notification icons that draw your attention to tips and important information to take note of as you read.

CALL NOTES

Call notes are typical questions you can ask the hiring manager or candidates while reviewing job descriptions or résumés.

TIPS

When you see this icon, pay close attention to the information and tips presented in this area.

SAMPLE

This icon shows you sample résumés or job descriptions for the job role being discussed.

QUESTIONS

This icon alerts you to special interview questions.

CONTACTING THE AUTHOR

If you have any questions regarding this book, need clarification, or simply want to offer your thoughts regarding *Technology Made Simple for the Technical Recruiter*, please feel free to send me an email at obi@ technicalrecruitingbook.com. To ensure your email goes to my in-box and not junk mail, please use the following in the subject line: "Thoughts on Technology Made Simple." I will do my very best to respond to you in a timely fashion.

Thank you for purchasing this book or reading just a few pages from it as you decide whether it will suit your needs. I hope you enjoy reading it and putting your newfound knowledge to use.

CHAPTER 1

THE TECHNICAL JOB REQUISITION

In This Chapter

- anatomy of a technical job requisition
- request for information from the hiring manager
- questions for the candidate based on the job requisition
- the recruiter's take

This book starts with the job requisition because it's the beginning of the process of recruiting. It's the purchase order, job order, or intent to purchase that a client provides to a recruiter that tells the recruiter the profile of the candidate to look for. In order to do this successfully, the recruiter needs to really understand what the client wants.

This chapter reviews a typical job requisition, analyzes the demands and skill sets for clarity, and then rates the possibility of finding a candidate that fits the requirements. We will also look at the link between the job requisition and a résumé to see when a résumé may have been edited to mirror skills from the job description and when a résumé truly represents the capabilities of the candidate.

In technical recruiting, as in most professions, the best practice is to stay within a defined area of expertise. Choose an area of technology to focus on and recruit candidates within this or closely related areas. By focusing on a specific area, the technical recruiter is able to dive deeply into that area to learn all there is to know. It also makes it easier for the recruiter to quickly review requisitions and identify (mis)matches. Areas of specialization may be based on specific vendors, such as CISCO and Oracle, or may be based on technology implementation phases, such as software development, software testing, database administration, network administration, and cloud configuration.

There are many reasons why you will want to understand the job requisition. The first reason is to be able to assure hiring managers that you understand their environment and their need and can locate a person for the current position and possibly others. The second reason is to be able to translate this understanding when describing the job role to a potential candidate. Whether you are a contract or corporate recruiter, you must be able to describe the position requirements to a candidate as if you were the hiring manager.

Anatomy of a Technical Job Requisition

When you review a job requisition, you should have a few questions in mind: questions pertaining to the platform, the network environment, the size of the company or number of users, the current team (if any), the level of expertise sought, any skills mismatch, and the experience of the hiring manager.

Let's take a look at the job requisition in figure 1.1, a sample SharePoint consultant's job description. A few of the questions above have been immediately identified and answered. For example, the level of expertise sought is senior level.

Hiring managers and their human resources representatives usually know what they want and spend time creating job descriptions that capture their wants and must-haves. Your job as the recruiter is to understand these wants, desires, and must-haves and to be able to isolate them in order to come up with a description that captures realistic demands (based on current talent pool and market forces) and attracts the right kinds of candidates.

When reviewing a job requisition, the first step is to underline or highlight every skill set. You can see these skill sets underlined in figure 1.1.

SAMPLE

<u>Senior</u> **SharePoint Consultant**

We have a need for a highly skilled <u>SharePoint</u> Consultant for our office. The primary focus for this position will be solution design, technology leadership, and application development in a SharePoint environment and other <u>Microsoft</u> and <u>.NET technologies.</u> The successful candidate will be responsible for gathering requirements, application design, database design, project team leadership, hardcore development, testing, and implementation.

Engagements range from enterprise portal implementations, extranet/VPN implementations, and 100 percent custom application development to <u>business intelligence</u>, data warehousing, <u>MS CRM customizations</u>, enterprise application integration, and more. Applicants must have a strong background in Microsoft development environments including <u>Visual Studio.NET</u>, <u>ASP.NET</u>, <u>VB.NET</u>, <u>C#</u>, and <u>MS SQL Server</u>. Applicants must have excellent <u>object-oriented development</u> skills, <u>documentation</u> skills, and project management expertise and must maintain a high level of professionalism.

Required Minimum Skills:
- Degree in the area of MIS, CIS, or computer science
- 5+ years minimum application development experience in a professional environment

---

- <u>1+ years of SharePoint experience (Designer)</u>
- 2+ years of .Net application development
- 3+ years of MS SQL Server
- database design skills
- object-oriented design skills

Desired Experience:
- Experience with Dynamics CRM, BizTalk or Commerce Server
- XML, XSL, Web services, and SOAP experience also a plus.
- Experience with Unified Modeling Language, Rational Methodology, or MCSD also considered a plus!

Figure 1.1. Sample SharePoint consultant job description

The second step is to start identifying answers to the main questions that revolve around the technology environment in the organization—answers that reveal the organization's platform, network environment, existence of legacy systems, number of users, level and type of expertise, and current team.

The platform: During review, you must identify the platform, which is usually the main environment in the company. From this requisition, we can identify that this company is a Microsoft shop; this means that the company requesting the SharePoint consultant has a major investment in Microsoft technologies.

How do we know that? It's revealed through the mention of Microsoft technologies all over the job description—.NET, SharePoint, Microsoft SQL Server, BizTalk, Visual Studio, Microsoft CRM, Silverlight, and Microsoft certification. All these point to the fact that this company is heavily invested in Microsoft. Therefore, to answer the platform question, you can clearly see that this is a Microsoft platform shop. Because the client is a big Microsoft user, it is also possible that a partnership may exist between the client and Microsoft. One of the requirements for a Microsoft partnership is that a company employ a given number of Microsoft-certified individuals. This may account for the desired requirement for the requested candidate to possess a Microsoft certification (more on certifications in chapter 13).

Network environment: Once the platform is identified, identifying the network environment is simple, as it is just an extension of the platform environment. In our example requisition, we identified the platform as Microsoft; this should point to the fact that this client uses Microsoft network operating systems (more on operating systems in chapter 5).

Interoperability with legacy systems: The requisition does not identify any legacy systems in its environment. However, you cannot conclude from this that the client does not have any legacy systems. It just indicates that this is an area that must be clarified with the hiring manager with a question like "Do you have any legacy systems in your environment or any non-Microsoft applications that require interfacing with the current Microsoft applications?"

Number of users: Some requisitions give you an indication of how many users are in an environment; our current example does not, so it needs to be clarified with the hiring manager with a question like, "How many users are in your SharePoint environment?" The answer to this question should tell you how many SharePoint users the selected candidate will support. The answer to this question should also help create a picture in your mind, which can be used when describing the environment to your potential candidates. Another question you may consider asking to ascertain user growth is, "What is your plan for migrating additional users to SharePoint in the future?"

Level of expertise: Notice that although the requisition is requesting a senior SharePoint consultant, the reference to direct SharePoint experience is "1+ years of SharePoint experience." This may seem like a mismatch in that the client is seeking a senior consultant in SharePoint but requires only about one year of experience in the software itself. However, reviewing the job requisition further, you will see that the client is looking for a core .NET developer with some experience in

SharePoint software. The main development area will be the SharePoint software—hence, the title of SharePoint consultant. While the current title may be popular, a more accurate title to engage prospective candidates may be .NET developer (SharePoint).

Type of expertise: This requisition has the title senior SharePoint consultant. The consultant title is usually a confusing one because it can mean different things to different people, so it's wise to clarify the intent from the hiring manager. A consultant can focus on one of three things—development, administration, or project management. It is clear that this requisition refers to a consultant that is focused on the development phase because of the requirement for development skills and experience in software development tools such as Visual Studio. NET, ASP.NET, VB.NET, and C#.

Current team: The requisition alludes to the fact that there are people with different skill sets in this company. These skill sets include portal implementations, extranet/VPN implementations, custom application development, business intelligence, data warehousing, MS CRM customizations, and application integration. This sounds like a consulting company that has engagements with other companies. For some candidates, this may seem like an ideal company where candidates are exposed to different work environments and industries from month to month and where they are never bored. For other candidates, this may be a nightmare position if the candidate is one that prefers a workplace that allows new hires the time and opportunity to learn from teammates. This is not always the case in consulting environments.

Request for Information (RFI)

After careful review of the job requisition, it is time to compile the list of questions and clarifications directed at the hiring manager. The purpose of the request for more information is twofold: to obtain clarification of any ambiguity as well as to confirm your understanding of the needs of the hiring manager. The clarification may include questions not answered by the job requisition, questions that may be asked by potential candidates with regard to the position, and questions to ascertain the most important skills and what makes for the near-perfect candidate.

It may sound as if you are preparing to interview the client when you start compiling these questions. In reality, you are. Figure 1.2 illustrates RFI questions for the hiring manager. Their purpose is to provide you with as much information as possible about the job in order to help you find the right candidate.

Request for Information
Senior SharePoint Consultant

(1) The three most important skills: (a)_____
(b) _____ (c)_____

(2) Average workweek expectation: a) 40hrs/week, b) 50hrs+/week, c) 55hrs+/week

(3) If presented with two great candidates, what skills will tilt your preference to hire one over the other?

(4) What is the average frequency of code prop to production, including hot fixes?

(5) Latest technologies implemented in your application: (a)_____ (b) _____ (c)_____

(6) How many development tiers are present in your applications?

Figure 1.2. Sample request for more information

Three most important skills: When reviewing a job requisition, you must identify the three most important skills in order of importance to the hiring manager. If you are recruiting in an area of focus (e.g., software development), you probably already know the three most important skills, although they still need to be confirmed with the hiring manager. This will help you identify the required baseline for potential candidates and help qualify and eliminate candidates quickly.

Average workweek expectation: This is an important question to ask the hiring manager. It's important because there are candidates who will not work more than a specified number of hours per week, give or take two hours here and there. There are also employers who require (albeit indirectly) their employees to work an average of fifty hours per week. This may seem irrelevant, but it has caused a number of employees to leave an otherwise great job for another. This also relates to the next question; what is the pace of the company?

Pace: It's almost a given that a technology or an online company is fast paced, although some are faster paced than others. Therefore, it's imperative that you ask the hiring manager about the pace of the company.

"What is the average frequency of code prop to production, including hot fixes?"

CALL NOTES

The pace of the company can be identified in the following way for a software development or web-based company. You want to find out the frequency of code propagation in their production environment by asking this question (meaning how many times they move new and updated programming code into their production servers, including hot fixes—software fixes of broken code): "What is the average frequency of code prop to production, including hot fixes?" The answer will tell you the number of cycles of code a software developer or tester goes through per week. The range of possible answers from the hiring manager includes "Once a week," "Twice a week plus one or two hot fixes," "Once every two weeks," or "Once a month."

Latest technology implementation: Most developers enjoy and look forward to working with the latest technologies or methodologies. For that reason, it would be good information to share with the candidate if you, as the recruiter, know that the client has implemented any project using the latest technologies. The possibility of working with the best and latest technology is an attractive option for the candidate. Here is how to frame your question to obtain the answers you seek.

CALL NOTES

"In terms of technology, what are the latest technologies your department has implemented in any of your projects? How deliberate are you in upgrading to the latest versions of software?"

Development tier: For the purpose of division of labor, application development can be divided into many layers, such as presentation, business logic, data access, and database. (See figure 1.3 for how these layers are separated.) A key benefit of keeping these application layers separate is that it allows parallel development of the different tiers of the application. One developer can work on the presentation tier while another builds the business tier and another works on the database tier.

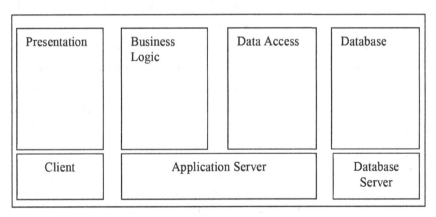

Figure 1.3. Multitier development

Working on separate tiers also allows for less complicated maintenance and support. This is because it's simpler to change and upgrade a single specific component than to make changes in a one-tier application. If the business rules of a multitier application are changed, it's only necessary to change the software logic in the business tier on one server.

With this in mind, seasoned developers prefer working on multitier applications, where every layer has been separated. It's easier to update and troubleshoot. So, as a recruiter, you want to find out from the hiring manager (who is looking for a developer) the development tier in place in their organization. Here is how to frame your question to obtain the answers you seek.

CALL NOTES

"In your development team, how do you separate the team members who work on a particular development tier? How many development tiers are present in your applications?"

Structured or ad hoc–driven process: Some technology organizations are more process driven than others; in these organizations, documentation and written processes are used for streamlining projects and for every change request. Some candidates would want to know if this is the case for the target organization. In my work experience as a developer, I have performed better when there has been a generally understood way to write code. This does not mean that a developer couldn't deviate occasionally, but it does mean that there is uniformity in how things are done. With all the information you have gathered about the position and the organization, you may become the recruiter of choice for the organization. Here is how to frame your question to obtain the answers you seek.

CALL NOTES

"What process or standards do you use for documentation, code generation, code review (peer-to-peer review of a developer's code), and version control? Do you have standards that everyone must follow, or is it a mixed ad hoc/structured environment?"

Criteria for choosing one out of two: There are those occasions where all you have for a job requisition is one candidate; this question would definitely not work there. However, on those occasions where you have two or three promising candidates for a job, you would want to know the hiring manager's criteria for choosing one person out of the two or three candidates presented. Whatever the answer is, it will help you fine-tune your search. Ultimately, you want to save your client's time and make the choice easy for the manager by finding two or three great candidates from which the hiring manager can pick one. The converse is to inundate the hiring manager with ten candidates, nine of which must be rejected, resulting in diminished confidence in your abilities as a recruiter. Here is how to frame your question to obtain the answers you seek.

CALL NOTES

"If you had two or three great candidates who fulfill your requirements, what would make you choose one over the other?"

Certifications or no certifications: As noted earlier in this chapter, there may be a specific reason why an organization requires certification, such as a partnership with a software vendor where the client organization is required to have one or two personnel with certain certifications. This is the case for Microsoft partnerships. Another reason may be that the client organization just wants to ensure that the candidate has done due diligence in a certain technical expertise. Speaking from experience, I was previously certified as a Microsoft Certified Database Administrator (MCDBA) in SQL Server and as a Microsoft Certified Business Management Solutions Professional (MCBMSP) in Microsoft Dynamics CRM. Those were tough exams to pass. The study and practice involved were painful, but I'm happy I obtained those certifications because they represented the foundational skills required in the job role. Possessing such certifications presents a value proposition to hiring managers that demonstrates the candidate's competency.

Whatever the reasons for an organization's certification requirement, you will want to know them. If no special reasons exist, then the job requisition may be better served if this requirement is removed. For candidates who have this certification, it's a foot in the door for them; however, there are candidates who may lack the certification, but who have in-depth experiences that satisfy all the other requirements. These candidates may be turned off by an organization's insistence upon certification (for more on certifications, see chapter 13). Here is how to frame your question to obtain the answers you seek.

CALL NOTES

"Is there a specific need for the certification requirement in your job description that I should know of? Do you need it to prove the competency of the candidate, or do you have a software vendor partnership requirement to fulfill?"

Job Requisition—with All the Answers

With all the questions answered, you are now ready to create a customized job description. This description may form a part of the job description you post on internet job boards or send to interested candidates. Whichever is the case, you have a job description that is different from the original and different from that created by most recruiters engaged by the client for the same job. Your job description has more information, and it is information that's important in attracting the right kinds of candidates. See figure 1.4 for a customized job description that includes additional information for candidates.

SAMPLE

Senior .NET Developer (SharePoint)

We have a need for a highly skilled .NET Developer for our SharePoint deployment—which is a 5000+ user SharePoint environment with plans to continue growing. The primary focus for this position will be solution design, technology leadership, and application development in a SharePoint environment and other <u>Microsoft</u> and <u>.NET technologies.</u> The successful candidate will be responsible for gathering requirements, application design, database design, project team leadership, hardcore development, testing, and implementation.

You will be working for a consulting company with client engagements that range from enterprise portal implementations, Extranet/VPN implementations, new development, and 100 percent custom application development to <u>business intelligence</u>, data warehousing, <u>MS Dynamics CRM customizations</u>, enterprise application integration, and more. Applicants must have a strong background in Microsoft development environments, including <u>Visual Studio.NET</u>, <u>ASP.NET</u>, <u>VB.NET</u>, <u>C#</u>, and <u>MS SQL Server</u>. Applicants must have excellent <u>object-oriented development</u> skills, <u>documentation</u> skills, and project management expertise and must maintain a high level of professionalism.

Required Minimum Skills:
- Degree in the area of MIS, CIS, or computer science
- 5+ years' minimum application development experience in a professional environment
- <u>1+ years of SharePoint experience</u>
- 2+ years of .Net application development
- 3+ years of MS SQL Server
- Database design skills
- Object-oriented design skills

Desired Experience:
- Experience with Silverlight, Dynamics CRM, BizTalk, or Commerce Server
- XML, XSL, ETL, Web services, and SOA experience a plus
- Experience with Unified Modeling Language, Rational Methodology a plus
- MCSD not required but considered a plus

Figure 1.4. Customized job description

Candidate Questions

From the review of the job requisition and the additional information received from the hiring manager, you are now able to draw up a list of questions that you will use to qualify and shortlist potential candidates for this job requisition. You may consider sharing this question list with the hiring manager; doing so ensures that the two of you are on the same page and also creates the impression that you know your work. This further builds the hiring manager's confidence in your ability to find the right candidate. Sharing your questions may also encourage the hiring manager to add additional questions to your list. This assumes that you have found some candidate résumés that fulfill the main requirements in the job requisition. You are now ready to call your candidates. Below is a script of your questions.

QUESTIONS

The recruiter may start by going through the preliminaries of basic recruiter and candidate greetings and then flow right into the interview.

Greeting:

Hello, Jim. My name is Nadine Clarke with ABC Consulting. I was referred to you by a mutual acquaintance (name the person if you have their permission) and wanted to speak with you about an opportunity that might interest you. Do you have a minute? (Get their permission to continue.)

Good. I have a .NET SharePoint development opportunity in Dallas, Texas, that's looking for someone with your set of skills. It's for a consulting company with client deployments that ensure its employees are never bored. These deployments are for enterprise portal implementations, new development, custom application development, business intelligence, data warehousing, Microsoft Dynamics CRM customizations, and enterprise application integration.

I'm going to ask you a few questions if that's okay with you. (Get their permission to continue.)

1. In your experience in .NET development, which development tier do you prefer to work with?
2. What does your average workweek look like?
3. How many code cycles or prop cycles do you typically go through in a week or month? {follow-up question} How would you change that if you could?
4. Which of the .NET components do you prefer to work with: C#, VB.NET, or ASP.NET?
5. Tell me a little about your input in creating a process-driven or methodology-driven development environment—you know … like documentation, code review process, unit testing, etc.
6. SharePoint is the main focus of development for this job. Would you mind sharing with me a customization or development project you've handled in the past on SharePoint? Please start with the problem and the process you went through to complete the project.

For more specific questions on SQL Server, see chapters 9 and 10. In the next chapter, we take a look at the candidate's résumé and compare it against the job requisition in order to formulate more questions for the candidate.

Possibility Rating

Having obtained answers to the RFI from the hiring manager and also affirmative answers to the candidate questions from the candidate, the technical recruiter is well on the way to finding the best candidate for the .NET Developer (SharePoint) position.

Considering the candidate questions and the information from the RFI, table 1.1 shows candidate answers that indicate a good fit for this position.

Questions	Possible Answers
(1) In your experience in .NET development, which development tier do you prefer to work with?	"I have worked on all the tiers at one time or other—the presentation, business logic, data access, and database layers. Sometimes the layer I'm working on depends on the project—how familiar I am with the project and whether the project time frame allows for ramp-up time."
(2) What does your average workweek look like?	"On an average, I work 45 to 50 hours per week, sometimes less."
(3) How many code cycles or prop cycles do you typically go through in a week or month? {follow-up question} How would you change that if you could?	"We prop every Wednesday. For the type of environment and business we are in, I think that frequency is appropriate."
(4) Which of the .NET components do you prefer to work with: C#, VB.NET, or ASP.NET?	"I have experience on all of them, but C# is the one I work with most of the time."

Table 1.1. Possible candidate answers

These questions are obviously only a subset of the questions that can be asked of a candidate based on the job description illustrated above. However, with the answers above, the possibility rating for this candidate may be between 80 and 85 over one hundred (80–85/100).

What We Learned

- When you review a job requisition, you should identify questions that you can ask of the hiring manager. These include questions about the platform, the network environment, the size of the company or number of users, the current team (if any), the level of expertise sought, and any skills mismatches.
- The request for information (RFI) is the list of questions directed at the hiring manager in order to gain clarification of any job description ambiguity and to confirm your understanding of the needs of the hiring manager.
- A customized job description different from the original was created based on the answers received from the hiring manager and the RFI.
- Candidate questions directed at validating the skills of the candidate were created. These questions were derived from the results of the answers to the RFI.

CHAPTER 2

THE TECHNICAL RÉSUMÉ

In This Chapter

- deciphering the résumé
- relationship between the résumé and the requisition
- questions from a résumé
- skill embellishment

What is a résumé, and why is it important? It's a candidate's product information, their brochure of services, their billboard, and the closest a recruiter can get to knowing a person without actually meeting them. The résumé can be an ally when written properly and can be an enemy of progress if written badly. As a recruiter, you have probably seen hundreds of résumés and can readily rate them "good," "bad," and "ugly" at a moment's glance. There are some résumés that jump out at you, saying, "Look at me," and some that just plainly whisper, "You can pass me by now." When you look at a résumé, there is some information you want to immediately see on the first page—information such as contact information, job title, summary of skills, and education.

In this chapter, we break down a résumé, making sure that all the parts that make up a well-written résumé are present, and then we derive questions from that résumé; résumés almost always leave some questions unanswered when reviewed for a specific job requisition. We will also find a link between a résumé and the job requisition and look for skill embellishments or "orphaned skills"—skills with no accompanying experience. Yes, a hiring manager may be happy to know that a candidate has experience in SharePoint Server, but it's also important to know where the candidate got that experience, aside from their home server network.

In this chapter, you will learn how to create content for those skills that may have been omitted from the candidate's résumé but for which the candidate actually has professional experience. This chapter will illustrate how this can be accomplished with authenticity.

Deciphering the Résumé

Reviewing a technical résumé for a specific job requisition will be easier once you have gone through chapter 1 of this book (where the job requisition was reviewed) and after the hiring manager has answered some questions about his or her needs in relation to the requisition. We will review the résumé in figure 2.1 for the .NET developer / SharePoint consultant position shown in chapter 1.

TIPS

Please note that some keywords are underlined to call your attention to them. We'll use the underlined skills to find out more about the candidate's experience.

SAMPLE

Steven Irmalaxi
SharePoint Senior Consultant

Steven's primary area of expertise is developing and implementing SharePoint collaboration portals and .NET web applications. He led the development of SharePoint portal technologies for the ABC Company, Origins Inc., and RPI Inc. Functional areas of expertise are systems integration and architecture, enterprise collaboration data management, and information security.

Technical Skills Summary

O/S	Windows 10, Microsoft Windows Server
Languages	.NET (C#, VB, and ASP), Java, XML, and SQL
Databases	SQL Server 20xx and 20xx
Other	SharePoint Server, Team Foundation server, Visual Studio, Visual Studio Team Services, Rational Suite, SharePoint Designer, Microsoft Office 365

Professional Experience

ABC Consulting   June 2010–Present

Senior Consultant (SharePoint and .NET Developer)

- SharePoint developer for SharePoint applications and sites.
- Led the development of an Enterprise Content Management System using SharePoint Designer, InfoPath, and .NET technologies. The enterprise system enables real-time collaboration across multiple locations.
- Developed critical data management systems for utilizing SharePoint Server and other technologies to enhance functionalities.
- Customized and configured site pages to target content to specific users.
- Developed custom workflows for approval of pages, created sites, and managed permissions and content.

CXD Company   December 2003–April 2010

Senior Consultant (SharePoint and .NET Developer)

- Lead developer on the CXD Information Management System for the utilization of SharePoint 2013 and .NET custom web parts and applications.

- Developer for a customized project management system utilizing SharePoint portal and integrating it with .NET applications and Microsoft Project Server 2016.
- .NET software developer building custom web applications integrating into suite of tools that were displayed as a digital dashboard for the end user using SharePoint 2013 technologies. This was an all-encompassing system streamlining all business processes across the division.
- Lead developer for a web-based .NET application maintaining and coordinating domestic and international travel agendas, itineraries, and research.

Education

<u>Bachelor of Science</u>, computer information systems, June 2003, New York State University

Certification: Microsoft Certified Solution Developer (<u>MCSD</u>)

Figure 2.1. Sample SharePoint résumé

At first glance, it's easy to see that Steven has all the skills that are required for this position. It's a résumé made in heaven for the SharePoint job requisition. But don't hurry to send Steven's résumé to the hiring manager. Remember the questions about pace, average workweek, and the type of company? The answers to all those questions must be ascertained before you can say that Steven is a match for the hiring manager's company.

If the hiring manager's and Steven's answers look like the suitability matrix in table 2.1, then you may reconsider Steve's suitability for this position.

Question	Hiring Manager	Steven
Type of company	Fast-growing IT consulting company.	Traditional company where he can learn and teach others; very family oriented.

Average week/ pace	55+ hours per week, sometimes more.	40 hours per week with the occasional two hours here and there.
Prop cycle	Twice a week with one or two hot fixes per week.	Once a month; on some occasions, twice a month. Hot fixes are inevitable, but they are at the minimum.
Process	Have processes used maybe 65 percent of the time; sometimes the urgent need for a hot fix trumps the need to follow the process.	Process is utilized 90 percent of the time.

Table 2.1. Suitability matrix

Steven is obviously not suitable for this position; other situations may influence him to accept this position, but he may not last more than a year in this company before he starts looking for another position more suitable to his lifestyle.

The bottom line when reviewing a résumé for a match with a job requisition does not begin and end with technical skills. Yes, it may start with the technical skills, but other factors are as important as the skills match. With all this in mind, let's look at parts of this résumé, including the candidate's overview, skills summary, education and certifications, and professional experience.

The candidate's overview: This is a summary of who the candidate is and what he or she is good at.

Skills summary: This section of the résumé is like the glossary of skills terms, the nutshell overview of all the skills and technologies that this candidate has worked with. This is the portion of the résumé that attracts the recruiter's eye, where the recruiter finds a list of all or some of the skills sought after.

Education and certifications: Education is important and usually found on the first page of the candidate's résumé. Most technical jobs now require a minimum of a bachelor's degree, so it's important the fulfillment of this requirement be placed on the front page.

Professional experience: Usually starts at the bottom of the first page and spans the rest of the résumé pages.

Relationship between the Requisition and Résumé

As a recruiter, you may send a job description to a candidate and request a résumé in return. Some candidates may, upon reviewing the job description, update their résumé to match the skill set on the job description. This is usually not an issue; sometimes it takes a job description to remind a candidate of experience in an area that may have been omitted on a résumé. It becomes an issue when you identify sprinkles of the skills in the job description but no experience to substantiate those skills.

Let's look at the job requisition presented in chapter 1 and compare it to two different résumés. One is sprinkled with skills but has no evidence of experience, while the other has the requisite skills backed by experience. When reviewing a résumé, it is not enough to accept the summary of skills (the list of all technologies used by the candidate) as evidence of experience.

The technical recruiter should use the same summary of skills as a basis for an interview or conversation with the candidate. If a skills summary looks similar to an excerpt from Amber's résumé (shown below in figure 2.2), with no reference made to the same skills in the professional experience section, then you must find out more.

SAMPLE

> ### Amber Henderson
> ### SharePoint Consultant
>
> Amber has over twelve years of experience in information technology, with seven years of implementation and development experience with SharePoint as a subject matter expert.
>
> **Summary of Skills**
> *SharePoint*: Microsoft Office SharePoint Server, Windows SharePoint Services 3.0 (WSS 3.0), SharePoint Portal Server 2013, SharePoint Designer 2013
> *Programming*: .NET: ASP.NET, C#, VB.NET, Web services, SQL Server, Silverlight, CSS, XML, XSL, XSLT, Visual Studio.NET
> *Platforms*: Windows Server, UNIX/Linux, HP-UX, DOS, Mac OS
>
> **Professional Experience**
> SharePoint Consultant, ABC Company Inc.   2010–present
> - Developed custom functionality with SharePoint 2013; implemented corporate SharePoint sites for collaboration.
> - Created interactive web interface and was able to quickly add functionalities and reuse code.

Figure 2.2. Summary of skills sample with no evidence of professional experience

In finding out more, one of two things may become evident: either Amber does not have professional experience to back up the skills in the summary section, or she does but did not adequately include the experience in the professional experience section of her résumé.

To find out more, you may ask questions like "Please tell me more about your experience using C# or VB.NET for web development. Feel free to use a problem and solution-based scenario to describe how you used this skill."

CALL NOTES

TIPS

Please remember that it's not enough to create a summary of skills in which you include all the skills the candidate claims to have. You should always seek to substantiate those skills with actual experience.

Table 2.2 shows an example of what the responses may look like for each of the itemized skills. These answers can then be used to augment Amber's professional experience résumé section and ready it for presentation to the hiring manager.

Skills	Years	Candidate Response	Résumé Update
.NET Development with C#, VB.NET, ASP.NET	5	"Needed to add a scheduling component on our online applicant tracking software ATS."	"Using ASP.NET, C#, and SQL Server, I was able to develop a solution that integrated seamlessly with current ATS."
Visual Studio .NET	5	"Used this since my early development days; there really wasn't a choice for me because that was the framework of choice for the company I worked for."	"It provided a framework to create applications that utilized web services that were complementary to our current web-based ATS application."

SharePoint	2	"Wanted to ensure that our organization's six regional offices were working with current versions of documentation."	"Implemented a document management and workflow application based on Microsoft Office SharePoint Server. The solution reduced the volume and cost of handling paperwork by about 50 percent."
SQL Server/Database Design	5	"Microsoft database solution is the default choice when working with Microsoft technologies. We needed a database management system for storing the ATS data."	"Using SQL Server, I designed and implemented the database objects for the applicant tracking software."
Silverlight	1	"Wanted to develop a more interactive web user interface for our ATS application built on the Microsoft .NET Framework."	"Taking advantage of the flexibility of Silverlight on the .NET Framework, I was able to create an interactive web interface and was able to quickly add functionalities and reuse code."

BizTalk	1	"While working with a major bank that had partnered with another bank to provide back office capabilities to their customers, we needed a system to support reliable dataflow between the two organizations."	"We deployed Microsoft BizTalk Server, Microsoft BizTalk Accelerator, and InfoPath Services to provide interoperability with our bank and a partner bank."

Table 2.2. Possible responses from candidate

Adding Professional Experience

When reviewing résumés, you may find that a candidate does have the experience but just omitted adding these examples of hands-on experience to the professional experience section of the résumé. In this instance, the technical recruiter is to do one of two things: either ask the candidate to update the résumé to include the experience or update the résumé yourself to include the missing information using the responses received from the candidate during your conversation. Please obtain consent before and after you update or add to a candidate's résumé. Using the responses from table 2.2, the recruiter can update the candidate's résumé to include the omitted skills.

A sample of what the résumé might look like after the recruiter update appears in figure 2.3. You will notice that in addition to referencing the skill sets—ASP.NET, C#, SQL Server, Silverlight, and .NET Framework—we also added how these skills/tools were used.

Amber Henderson
SharePoint Consultant

Amber has over twelve years' experience in information technology, with seven years of implementation and development experience with SharePoint as a subject matter expert.

Summary of Skills

SharePoint: Microsoft Office SharePoint Server 2013, Windows SharePoint Services 3.0 (WSS 3.0), SharePoint Portal Server 2013, SharePoint Designer 2013

Programming: .NET: ASP.NET, C#, VB.NET, Web services, SQL Server, Silverlight, CSS, XML, XSL, XSLT, Visual Studio.NET

Platforms: Windows Server, UNIX/Linux, HP-UX, DOS, Mac OS

Professional Experience

SharePoint Consultant, ABC Company Inc.   2010–present

- Developed custom functionality with SharePoint API that integrated seamlessly with current system using ASP.NET, C#, and SQL Server.
- Created an interactive web interface and was able to quickly add functionalities and reuse code taking advantage of the flexibility of Silverlight on .NET Framework.

Figure 2.3. Summary of skills sample with added professional experience

Questions from a Résumé

Aside from the usual nontechnical questions that arise from reviewing a résumé, such as date discrepancies, years of experience for each skill, and why a candidate left a prior company, there are technical questions that may arise.

Looking at the SharePoint résumé in figure 2.1, the following are questions that a technical recruiter may ask a candidate to provide greater insight into the candidate's experience. The recruiter may start the conversation in the following way after going through the basic preliminaries of recruiter and candidate exchange.

"I'm going to ask you some general questions; your answers will give me a better understanding of what you do and perhaps what you enjoy the most in your job as a SharePoint consultant. Is that all right?"

- "Tell me about the MOSS and .NET-based Enterprise Content Management System. What problem did this solve? How long was the project? As a lead person, what would you have done differently to shorten the project time?"
- "As a lead role in this project, will you share the processes you went through to start and complete this project? What were the business considerations you made for some of the development work you did?"
- "How many other people were on your team? What were their roles?"
- "In addition to your development, testing, and production environments, did you also have staging and training environments? What role did the development team play in these other environments?"
- "What software did you use for version control? In these environments, who was responsible for moving the development code from development to the testing environment? Was this person part of your team too?"
- "What is the ratio of your lead role activities versus actual development: 50:50, 30:70, or what other ratio?"
- "How did you get into SharePoint technology?"

Please provide sufficient time for your candidate to respond fully before proceeding to ask another question.

TIPS

Skill Embellishments

Skill embellishment is the practice of including skills in a candidate's résumé in order to match the job requisition. Seasoned technical professionals with real-life professional experience will generally refrain from including skills on their résumé of which they know little or nothing. The best practice for a technical recruiter is to avoid including skills on a candidate's résumé unless the candidate has real-life work experience to back up the skills.

My colleague Mark once came out of an interview infuriated because the recruiter who sent him there had included many extra skills in the copy of his résumé sent to the hiring manager. After spending a few minutes fielding questions in areas in which he had little experience, he informed them that he had little interest in working as a database administrator.

He had thought the job opening was for a database engineer, not a database administrator (see the difference between database administrator and database engineer in chapter 10). No wonder he was asked several questions on backup/recovery and other database administration questions. After the interview, he requested to see the résumé that had been sent to the hiring manager; needless to say, it was heavily weighted with database administrator skills.

What We Learned

- The technical recruiter needs to decipher a technical résumé to determine the suitability of a candidate to a job description.
- In reviewing the link between a résumé and a job requisition, it is important to ask some simple questions such as "Would you tell me more about yourself?" Answers to such questions have a way of bringing out more information about the candidate. This

additional information can then be included in the candidate's résumé.

- It is common for a technical recruiter to have to add professional experience when it has been omitted in the professional experience section of the résumé.
- It is helpful to identify questions arising from a résumé that provide greater insight into the candidate's experience.
- Avoid skill embellishment, which is the practice of including skills on a résumé in order to match the job requisition, especially without the candidate's permission.

CHAPTER 3

THE TECHNOLOGY TEAM

In This Chapter

- the technology organization chart
- key role descriptions
- the recruiter's take

Whether you are a new technical recruiter or an experienced one, when introduced to a new client, you immediately want to know more about the company in terms of who the main contact person is and any important counterparts, the makeup of that person's team, and the role of the hiring manager along with his or her relevant reporting structure both above and below. In essence, you want to know more about your client.

In a technology group, there are many roles involved in the design, analysis, and implementation of a system. Software companies do not have typical IT departments in any real sense; this is because most aspects of jobs in this type of organization are technology based. Instead of the typical IT department, you find departments such as application development, database engineering, project management, and operations, where each main function is a full-fledged department complete with its own director and manager.

Nontechnology-based companies have traditional IT departments that report to either the chief finance officer (CFO) or chief information officer (CIO).

The Technology Organization Chart

Unless the roles played by people in a group are obvious, the recruiter should seek to understand the hierarchy of authority in each group. The natural inclination of most people after being introduced to a family is the need to find out (albeit indirectly) who wields more authority in the relationships.

The technical recruiter should follow this same inclination when faced with a new client. As the relationship between the recruiter and a company develops, the recruiter needs to figure out who reports to whom, where everyone fits, and factors affecting the decision to select a new hire. This information becomes crucial when the organization begins to decide which of your candidates is the best fit for a position.

Using a pencil and paper and beginning with the CIO title is a good way to start creating an organization chart for your new clients. As your relationship continues to grow, you will be able to ask your contact hiring manager questions to find out who the other influencers are.

"Who else is involved with the hiring process in your group?" "Is there anyone else with whom you would like me to discuss the job requirements?"

CALL NOTES

Armed with the information you collect during this process, you will know who has the last word, who the directors are, and who their direct reports are. The information you acquire here can help you create new relationships with other directors and managers who may also need your expertise in the future.

You may have created a perfect organization chart for your client organization at one time or another, but it's important to keep one thing in mind: things change all the time, and people tend to change positions and companies. To ensure that the organization chart you create stays relevant, it must include phone extensions, job titles, and first and last names. That way, when the inevitable change does come, the name may change, but the title and phone extensions will most likely be retained.

Tech123.com (An Online Company)

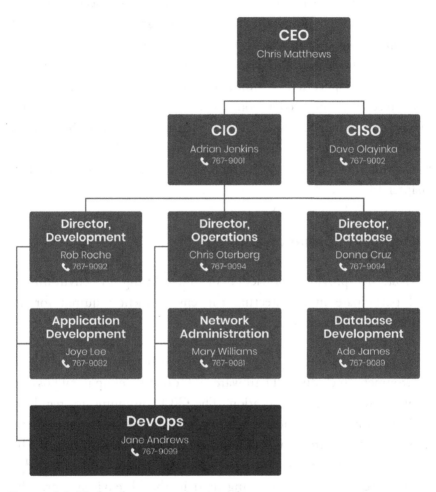

Figure 3.1. Technology organization chart

Figure 3.1 shows the organization chart for a typical technology consulting company specializing in implementing business solutions for its clients. Here we review some job titles and roles as presented in the organization chart for the CIO, chief information security officer (CISO), managers, business analysts, project managers, developers, and DevOps involved in providing services to its clients. You may notice that the CIO title is on the same hierarchical level as the CISO. Given the growing importance of information security in organizations, this role is receiving more recognition. Organizational structure differs from one organization to the next. In some organizations, the CISO reports to the CIO, whereas in others, the CISO and CIO are on the same level. More information about the role of the CISO can be found in chapter 13.

CIO (Chief Information Officer)

Purpose: To provide knowledge of the existing IT environment and participate in architecting the environment required for all implementation projects.

Description: The CIO is responsible for the organization's entire IT environment, including all hardware and software set up in all possible locations within the organization. The CIO communicates regularly with the unit or department directors/managers during system analysis and the architecture design of any new hardware and software. The CIO has a good understanding of the organization and knowledge of the specific applications being used in the IT environment. The CIO is familiar with all the department heads and users who will be affected by any new implementation. The CIO should have a thorough understanding of the impact project decisions have on the IT infrastructure. This person acts as a resource to the directors.

Functional/technical skills: The CIO should have detailed understanding of the technologies under his or her management and thorough knowledge of all the organization's related technologies. The CIO has fundamental understanding of all business systems within the organization as well as a good understanding of project methodology, business models, and data models for system implementation. The CIO has general IT knowledge and the ability to learn and understand new technologies.

Typical activities: The CIO reviews, approves, or disapproves all planning and proposal documents; contributes to infrastructure analysis and design and makes the decisions on hardware and software within the organization; supports decisions concerning business and financial aspects; and supports negotiation and finalization of contracting documents for any technical project implementation.

CISO (Chief Information Security Officer)

Purpose: To define, manage, and monitor all aspects of the organization's information security functions. Also responsible for developing and maintaining an information security governance, risk, and compliance (GRC) program.

Description: The CISO is responsible for the organization's information security profile. Oversees all aspects of information security and manages four main security components in the organization: security engineering, security operations center, emergency and incident response management, and program management. See chapter 13 for more detail.

Functional/technical skills: The CISO possesses combined experience in risk management, information security, and IT. He or she has comprehensive understanding of security risk management as well as standard risk frameworks, such as NIST, PCI, HIPAA, ISO, and SANS, and is usually certified with CISSP, CISA, or an equivalent credential.

Typical activities: The CISO develops and implements a strategic plan for governance, risk, and compliance; participates in the identification of security risks; develops and implements security management plans to mitigate risks; and defines metrics to monitor and measure security incidents and performance.

Director, Application Development

Purpose: To manage development managers and their staff, oversee application development projects, and provide mentorship and leadership to development staff.

Description: The breadth and depth of knowledge and experience in a wide range of application development methodologies of the person in this role give him or her the ability to see the big picture in any development project and create development best practices. This person acts as a resource to managers.

Functional/technical skills: The director of application development has demonstrated ability to lead multiple application development teams; has demonstrated experience managing the support and enhancement of software; and is able to take ownership of multiple applications and accurately report schedules and status. Significant project management experience gives the director of application development the ability to manage and prioritize product requirements, including the ability to create accurate project plans. He or she has a good understanding of software architecture and the ability to work with lead engineers at a technical level to design flexible, scalable, and secure systems and also possesses good working knowledge of traditional and agile development methodologies as well as a general knowledge of systems (e.g., various programming languages, databases, system and network architectures, design patterns). Web development experience is a plus, as is technical proficiency in the .NET + SQL Server, Java + MySQL, or other development framework plus database combinations.

Typical activities: The director of application development plans, leads, assigns, supervises, and controls activities related to software design and development; oversees multiple software engineering teams; is responsible for the design and development of numerous products; provides support to managers and their team members in order to meet the organization's functional and quality requirements; and identifies and recommends technical options. The individual in the director role participates in the analysis and development of business requirements.

Director, Database Development

Purpose: To manage the organization's database development. The director of database development oversees database development projects, creates best practices for database development, and acts as a support to database development staff.

Description: The director of database development oversees database engineers, data architects, and data analysts; coordinates physical changes to databases, codes, and tests; and implements numerous databases by applying knowledge of database management.

Functional/technical skills: The director of database development has thorough understanding and experience of database system operating characteristics, their capabilities and limitations, and knowledge of their architecture, administration, infrastructure, and database systems tools. He or she also has knowledge of multiple operating systems, such as Linux, UNIX, and Microsoft Windows; has knowledge of the methodologies for data modeling in the design and creation of tables, relationships, indexes, unique constraints, and capacity requirements; is skilled in database performance-tuning techniques, database security, and auditing functions; and is also knowledgeable in client/server technology, architecture, software development life cycle, and other standards.

Typical activities: The director of database development coordinates, supervises, and monitors the work of database developers; plans and prepares performance reviews; hires and trains new personnel;

reviews and approves database management system configuration recommendations; and oversees the development and organization of databases. This person recommends tools to assist in the management of database development, testing, staging, and production environments.

Director, Operations

Purpose: To manage technology operations, including the setup and implementation of hardware, network, and telecommunications infrastructure in an organization.

Description: The director of operations manages the configuration of network hardware and software. The role also coordinates the implementation of security best practices and strategies. Production database administrators may often be found under the supervision and direction of the director of operations, who communicates with the CIO and other business unit directors. The director of operations provides an infrastructure technology vision to all business units and always seeks to provide cost-effective infrastructure solutions that reduce the total cost of ownership.

Functional/technical skills: The director of operations has thorough understanding of technology operations and best practices, as well as sound understanding and experience in contract negotiation and vendor management for software acquisition. He or she has good knowledge of the system development life cycle and project management practices. He or she is experienced in a broad range of applications, databases, and technologies areas, including enterprise systems such as UNIX, AIX, Solaris, Linux, J2EE, and Windows Server; end user systems such as desktops, laptops, and mobile devices; and hardware and systems related to global wide area networks / local area networks that connect different office locations. The director of operations has a broad experience in systems management and information security operations as well as in managing the implementation of operational tools and processes for firewalls, IDSs, IPSs, VPNs, and other security-related technologies.

Typical activities: The director of operations oversees the design and implementation of standards for local and wide area network infrastructure; selects, evaluates, and hires personnel; works with senior management to recommend and establish technology and business strategy; manages vendor relationships to obtain the best possible terms for the organization; and ensures that budgets and schedules meet corporate requirements.

Business Analyst

Purpose: To review business processes in order to gain a complete understanding of current procedures, identify improvements, document those processes, and connect business people to information technology groups in an organization.

Description: The business analyst is responsible for analyzing and modeling existing business processes. The goal of business process analysis is to understand and document current business procedures and identify areas for improvement. A thorough understanding of the current state of the organization is necessary prior to recommending changes related to implementing a new business solution. The business analyst uses modeling tools to document the current state of business processes as well as the desired future state and is responsible for the knowledge transfer of business implications to application/database developers and project managers.

Functional/technical skills: The business analyst has business analysis skills and experience in modeling business processes; has good documentation skills; knows how to conduct workshops and training sessions; and has good industry knowledge.

Typical activities: The business analyst prepares for and conducts business process analysis, documents and presents analysis and modeling results, and transfers knowledge to application/database developers and project managers.

Project Manager

Purpose: To schedule and coordinate project resources and ensure that time and budget targets are being met.

Description: The project manager is responsible for ensuring that all aspects of a project are planned and executed in a manner that meets the implementation goals within an established time frame and budget. The project manager should have a thorough understanding of the product being developed, ensuring that all technical resource persons are performing within the established project plan.

Functional/technical skills: With a fundamental understanding of related technologies, the project manager has experience with the management of risk, change, issues, time, scope, resources, budget, and quality. He or she also possesses knowledge of methodology and best practices; has experience with Microsoft Office Project and (or) other tools used for project management; and has a good understanding of all major activities for a system development life cycle implementation, such as analysis, design, development, and deployment.

Typical activities: The project manager scopes project phases; identifies and acquires resources for a project; conducts kickoff meetings; creates and maintains plans for all project activities; and participates in all application design and code review meetings. This is the go-to person for all status communications related to the project, who ensures that timelines are met and that the project is within budget while also ensuring that deliverables are built according to specification and are finished on time.

Application Developer (Lead)

Purpose: To provide both technical and functional knowledge of the product being implemented as well as all related technologies required for the implementation.

Description: The lead application developer is the primary resource for determining the approach to be utilized in a project implementation. The person in this role should possess a thorough understanding of the product from both a functional and technical perspective and have a comprehensive understanding of the implementation methodologies for the technology being utilized in product development, such as .NET or Java Framework. The lead application developer participates in every aspect of the development and implementation, working with business analysts to ensure full understanding of the change implications for current business processes. He or she designs and builds product deliverables according to specifications; escalates technical design or specification issues to the business analyst / project manager and application development director; works within a given time frame to complete coding; and follows good development practices and software development life cycle methodologies throughout product development.

Functional/technical skills: For a Microsoft Windows–based company, the lead application developer should be knowledgeable in Microsoft .NET technology; Microsoft Visual Studio development system; hardware sizing and architecture; network and operating systems; server technologies such as Microsoft SQL Server Database, reporting services, analysis services, N-tier architecture, and web servers; and internet technologies such as Microsoft Internet Information Server (IIS), Microsoft BizTalk Server, and firewalls.

Typical activities: In beginning phase, the activities of the lead application developer include estimations of technical and development tasks. In the analysis phase, they include analysis and validation of design. In the design phase, they include validation and review of design with peers and other developers for acceptance. In the development phase, they include the review of development and preparation for testing and deployment.

DevOps

Purpose: To accelerate the deployment and delivery of applications and services to clients using automation and streamlined processes, as well as to collaborate with both application development and IT operations teams to fully automate the build and release management processes.

Description: DevOps is the blending of "development" and "operations." The DevOps professional uses tools and practices from both the development and operations teams to deploy software and services to clients. He or she works under both departments and in several environments, such as development, test, and production. The main job of the DevOps is to rapidly deliver reliable services to clients.

Functional/technical skills: The DevOps professional should be knowledgeable about software development life cycles and have knowledge of software builds and releases and deployment to desktop, server, mobile, and web products. This person should be proficient in Linux, UNIX shell scripting, Perl, and Python and have experience with continuous integration tools such as Visual Studio Team Services (VSTS), Jenkins, and Microsoft Team Foundation Server (TFS), as well as configuration management tools such as Ansible, Chef, and Puppet.

Typical activities: The DevOps writes scripts to automate code builds, code testing, and the rapid deployment of software and services to clients while partnering and collaborating with all development and IT operations teams.

Why the Organization Chart

You may have had an experience of presenting a great candidate to a client who, after many interviews, turned your candidate down. The turndown may have been for many reasons, but one of the reasons may have been that the candidate did not meet a unique need of one of the key decision makers. For example, a member of the hiring team may have a bias toward candidates with certifications. As a result, that individual will automatically reject résumés without such certifications. This type of information can be collected when using an organization chart in order to show who the key decision makers are and what unique criteria they may be looking for beyond the technical requirements for the position.

You can use the organization chart to do several things, including identifying other potential clients within the organization and finding out who the influencers, directors, managers, and peers are who play a part in deciding who is hired and why. The important thing is to ask the hiring manager the following questions:

CALL NOTES

"Who is the candidate's primary customer?"

"Who will participate in the interview? Are these managers or peers?"

"Who else is involved in the selection process?"

The Recruiter's Take

There are many more titles and roles in a typical technology organization than are represented in figure 3.1. The chart is only an example of what you may start with when creating the organization chart of one of your clients. One of the objectives of the organization chart is to get a handle on who's who in an organization—their correct names, phone numbers, titles, and their ability to influence a decision.

There are simple ways to quickly create organization charts. You can use Microsoft Word or PowerPoint, or your current applicant tracking system (ATS) might already have this functionality.

- *Word / presentation application*: Microsoft Word and PowerPoint come with an intuitive tool called *SmartArt* for quickly creating professional organization charts. In either application, this tool is found in the *Insert* tab.
- *ATS*: Your organization may already have an ATS that includes organization chart creation. This process may work by requiring you to enter all the main contact persons for a certain client—CEO, CIO, HR director, and development director—with appropriate attributes such as first and last name, title, department, phone, email, etc. The ATS then creates an organization chart based on the information entered for a client organization.

You might consider asking the hiring manager to send you their organization's chart. I must warn you, however, that most companies are reluctant to release their organization charts to recruiters for obvious reasons—employee poaching and unsolicited cold calls.

TIPS

Whatever you do, don't send your candidates a blank organization chart template and require them to complete their company's organization chart for you. This usually turns the candidate off from further dealings with the recruiter. Creating the organization chart should really be the job of the recruiter.

What to Do with an Organization Chart

Now that we've discussed the reason for the organization chart and how to create one, let's move on to the things you can do with some of the contact information on the organization chart.

- Invite the contacts to connect with you through LinkedIn.
- Ask your hiring manager for permission to meet with some of the high-level persons on the organization chart or to set up a meeting with the other influencers.
- If you receive a negative response, seek to learn as much as you can about the other employees, such as their past schools, what they consider a good fit, and so on.

What We Learned

- The organization chart is an important tool in the recruiter's arsenal, helping the recruiter identify influencers at client organizations.
- In our study of a simple organization chart, we reviewed the job roles of the following titles:
    - o *CIO*: Responsible for the overall IT outlook in the organization and provides overall IT direction.

o *CISO*: Defines, manages, and monitors all aspects of the organization's information security functions. Also responsible for developing and maintaining an information security governance, risk, and compliance (GRC) program.

o *Director, application development*: Manages development managers and their staff, oversees application development projects, and provides mentorship and leadership to development staff.

o *Director, database development*: Manages the organization's database development. Oversees database development projects, creates best practices for database development, and acts as a support for database development manager and staff.

o *Director, operations*: Manages technology operations, including the setup and implementation of hardware, network, and telecommunications infrastructure in an organization.

o *Project manager*: Identifies and manages the project team and ensures that timelines are met and that the project is within budget.

o *Business analyst*: Reviews business processes to gain a complete understanding of current procedures; documents those processes and identifies improvements.

o *Application developer (lead)*: Provides both technical and functional knowledge of the product being implemented, as well as all related technologies required for the implementation.

o *DevOps*: Accelerates the deployment and delivery of applications and services to clients using automation and streamlined processes.

- Simple ways to quickly create organization charts include using Microsoft Word, PowerPoint, and your current ATS.
- We also discussed why the organization chart is important in discovering influencers and their decision-making processes during candidate selection.

CHAPTER 4

NETWORKING FUNDAMENTALS

In This Chapter

- from the beginning
- Open Systems Interconnection (OSI)
- categories of networks
- types of networks
- network protocols

From the Beginning

Computers can accomplish little without the ability to network with other computers and devices. The power of networking lies in its potential to connect different computers without barriers, to send and receive information along the network, and to share resources.

When you look at any software application, computer, or mobile device, you will find that they all have some form of networking capability. Networking enables computer users to share resources in order to save time and costs. Some uses of networking include the following: (1) file sharing, whereby files can be stored in a central location so that other users can access them; (2) printer sharing, by which multiple users share a printer, thereby saving the cost of purchasing individual printers; and (3) communicating through networks using mail and text services.

This chapter describes the types and uses of networks and the components and protocols that make up a network. The chapter also demonstrates the flow of information through a network and the protocols that enable the flow.

The Open Systems Interconnection (OSI) Network Model

In order to grasp the fundamentals of networking, the technical recruiter needs a basic understanding of the layers of a network, the protocols found in each layer, and how these layers interact. We will use the OSI model to illustrate networking. As defined by the International Standards Organization (ISO), the OSI model is a classification of network communication in a series of layers. It describes how the network layers interact.

The Seven Layers of the OSI Network Model

There are seven layers in this model: application, presentation, session, transport, network, data link, and physical. We will use communications between two users to describe the interaction between the layers. This pictorial representation shows data movements from one network layer to another.

o The *application layer* provides connection to a network using applications. The Outlook email application and database queries are examples of applications in this layer.
o The *presentation layer* takes the data from the application layer and presents it in a format that is understandable by computers. This layer also encrypts/compresses data in the origination layer and decrypts/decompresses data in the destination layer.
o The *session layer* opens and closes sessions between two computers during communication.
o The *transport layer* breaks down data into manageable segments and delivers them error-free and in the proper sequence.
o The *network layer* routes messages and data to the appropriate address along the best available path.
o The *data link layer* identifies the recipient computer on the network; this layer controls who has access to the physical network, eliminating possible confusion over the ownership of data.
o The *physical layer* is the actual physical connection between the computers. Devices such as hubs, routers, cables, and network adapters operate in this layer.

To describe the OSI model, we use an illustration of a typical instance of noncomputer network communication between two users. Kate is the message originator, and Donna is the recipient.

o Kate types a document.
o Kate puts it in an envelope, addresses it, and leaves it for mail pickup.
o The mail clerk picks up the envelope and delivers it to the mail room.
o The mail room staff reads the address and determines how to route the mail.
o After this determination, the staff places the envelope inside the appropriate box.
o The staff arranges for pickup.

The envelope is transported to the intended recipient in the following fashion.

- o The envelope is delivered to the mailroom of Donna's office.
- o The mailroom staff removes the outer box.
- o The staff then determine who the mail is for and sort it for delivery.
- o A mail clerk takes the mail to Donna's office and delivers the mail.
- o Donna opens the piece of mail and reads it.

Now look at a typical network communication between the same two people (see figure 4.1).

- o The transmission starts when Kate types an email message to Donna and presses the "send" key; this occurs in the *application layer*.
- o Kate's operating system appends to the message a packet (envelope) that identifies the sender and intended recipient(s); this occurs in the *presentation layer*.
- o The message is translated into a format that will be understandable by computers; this occurs in the *presentation layer*.
- o The message is then prepared for transmission and transport; this occurs in the *session, transport, network, data link,* and *physical layers.*
- o Adding delivery and reading of the message completes the journey of Kate's email.

The sequence of events for message delivery through a network is similar to a person-to-person communication. At each stage, header information is attached to the sent data and then stripped as it goes down the recipient's protocol stack.

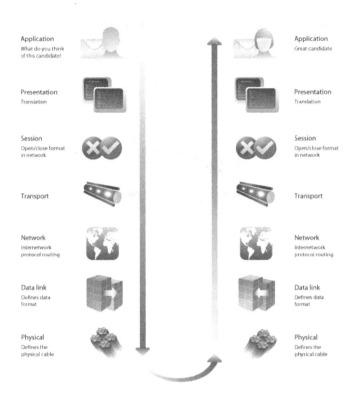

Figure 4.1. When two computers communicate, data passes up through the sender's protocols, across the network, and then down the recipient's protocol stack

Definitions of Server and Client

A *client* is a computer or application that receives information or resources from another computer. When a computer is making a request to another computer, the requesting computer is referred to as a *client*.

A *server* is a program or computer system that responds to and fulfills requests from client computers in a networked environment. When a computer is fulfilling a request, it is "serving"; therefore, it is referred to as a *server*. In some cases, computers can act as both a server and a client, making requests of other servers (as a client) and also fulfilling requests from other servers (as a server).

Figure 4.2. Network connections

The client and server computers are connected using network media such as cables, fiber optics, or wireless networking interfaces between the computer systems. A network adapter is a physical piece of hardware that allows your computer to connect to a network. Whether the networking media is cable, fiber optics, or wireless, the physical connection that we usually see is called a network adapter. For wireless network connections, this will be the wireless network card or wireless adapter.

Categories of Networks

Computer networks can be either peer-to-peer networks or server-based networks.

Peer-to-Peer Networks

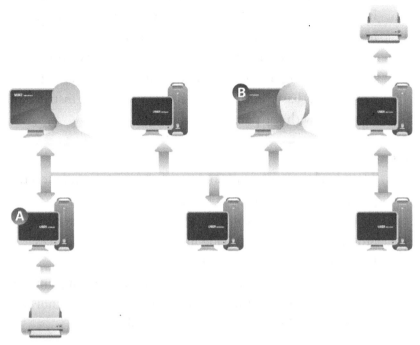

Figure 4.3. A peer-to-peer network

This is a type of network on which each computer acts as either a server (responding to requests), a client (requesting resources), or both. There is usually no centralized control of resources on this type of network.

Pros

o   Setup is fairly easy where all computers are linked together.

o   It is inexpensive because there is no need to purchase a separate network operating system or a server computer.

o   Maintenance is relatively easy because there is little or no network configuration that may require technical expertise beyond the basic information contained in the instructions that come with the purchased hardware.

Cons

o   There is a known decrease in the performance of computers that perform the role of a server in a peer-to-peer network.

o   Security is weak in this scenario. Users are not required to provide any credentials to log in or use network resources.

o   Decentralized resources could be difficult to manage. You may notice that in figure 4.3, the result of having a printer on computer (A) is that the person at computer (B) may not have access to printing when computer (A) is shut down.

Server-Based Network (Client/Server)

A *server-based network* is a network of computers that have a computer dedicated as a centralized controller of all the network resources. In a server-based network, the centralized computer is usually more sophisticated in terms of the internal processing resources it requires to satisfy requests generated by clients. For example, it requires a network operating system (NOS), such as Windows Server or UNIX. With the network operating system, users are configured in a domain structure requiring usernames and passwords to gain access to the network.

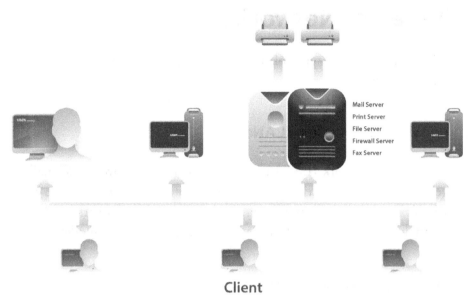

Client

Figure 4.4. A server-based network in which the server resources are centrally controlled

Pros

- o Security is controlled in a central location/server.
- o There is faster access to network resources; this is because the server has more processing power.
- o The server is always up and running, which ensures that resources are always available.

Cons

- o It's more expensive to implement a network; may require a systems administrator.
- o It involves network and user access configuration. Therefore, it is more complicated than a peer-to-peer network.
- o It requires the purchase of a network operating system (NOS).
- o It requires expensive server hardware.

Types of Networks

There are two main types of networks: local area networks and wide area networks.

Local Area Networks (LANs)

A local area network (LAN) is a computer network covering a small geographic area, such as a home, or one location, such as an office or school. Among LANs, there are wired and wireless networks. LAN technologies function at all the layers of the OSI reference model.

Wired Local Area Network

In a wired LAN environment, local computers on a network are connected through the use of cables or wires.

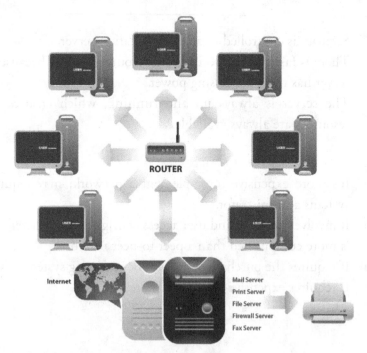

Figure 4.5. Wired LAN structure

Pros

- o *Security*: It is more difficult to break into a wired network than a wireless network.
- o *Speed*: The speed on a wired network is usually faster than on a wireless one.
- o *Reliability*: Wired networks have relatively stable network connectivity. It's unusual to experience dropped connectivity unless the cable is unplugged or you encounter other issues that may not be related to the reliability of the wired network.
- o *Cost*: If a home or office is prewired, then it is considered an easy installation.

Cons

- o *Cost*: In instances where the office needs to install new network jacks, the cost of ownership is higher than a wireless network.
- o *Setup*: It sometimes requires hiring a technician to wire and configure the network and security.
- o *Immobility*: Users on a wired network have limited mobility.

Wireless Local Area Network

On a wireless LAN, local computers are connected on the network without the use of cables or wires. This is typical in homes because it is easier to install. It can also be used in workplaces where employees are always in and out of meetings and need access to information on their computers. Workplaces could have a combination of wired and wireless networks, where each network (wired or wireless) has a purpose to fulfill.

Figure 4.6. A wireless peer-to-peer network

Pros

- o *Cost*: Given the ease of installation, the total cost of ownership of a wireless network is lower than a wired one.
- o *Ease of setup*: When installation directions are followed, it is easier to install in homes or small offices. Consequently, it may not require a support person.
- o *Mobility*: Users on a wireless network are able to move from room to room with their laptops with ease.

Cons

- o *Lack of security*: It is usually easier to breach the security of a wireless network than a wired network.
- o *Slow speeds*: Wireless networks are usually slower than wired ones.
- o *Unreliability*: Wireless technology is based on radio frequency, which results in higher rates of dropped network connectivity.

Wide Area Networks (WAN)

A WAN is a data communications network that is geographically separated. WAN technologies function mostly at the lower three layers of the OSI reference model (physical layer, data link layer, and network layer).

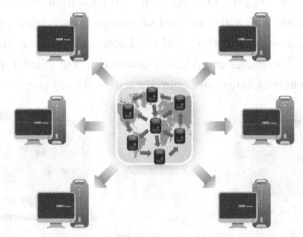

Figure 4.7. A wide area network (WAN)

WANs are mostly used by organizations that have multiple office locations that require a secure and cost-effective network solution for their employees to communicate and share information across a network. WANs are often used for centralizing transactions in retail or hospitality businesses. Wide area networks can be private or public, wired or wireless, and can be implemented using technologies such as remote access VPN or point-to-point connections.

Point-to-Point Connection

A point-to-point connection provides a single WAN communications path from one location to a remote network through a carrier network, such as a telephone company.

Figure 4.8. Point-to-point connection through a WAN to a remote network

Point-to-point lines are dedicated lines usually leased from a telephone company; therefore, such connections are more expensive than shared services. Figure 4.8 illustrates a typical point-to-point connection through a WAN.

Virtual Private Network (VPN)

The function of a VPN is to allow two computers or networks to talk to each other securely over a public and unsecure internet connection. VPNs rely on tunneling protocols to create a private network. Tunneling is the process of placing a data packet within another packet and sending it over a network. Figure 4.9 illustrates a remote access VPN connection.

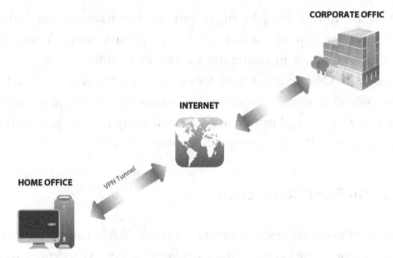

Figure 4.9. A remote access VPN connection

Although VPNs allow WAN connectivity through the internet at greatly reduced costs, this type of remote access connectivity is more susceptible to security risks. To ensure a level of security, VPNs must encrypt the data being passed through the public network and must also verify (authenticate) the computer on the other end.

Network Protocols

Protocols are rules that manage network communications between two computers. Listed below are some protocols you may have seen on some job descriptions and what they do. Protocols are categorized as either connection protocols or connectionless protocols.

Connection communication is similar to what happens when you make a telephone call. A call is initiated, a connection is established, and then you speak with a person at the other end. The connection is terminated when the conversation ends. This type of connection is used in WAN environments where there needs to be an established connection between two or more devices. This is generally referred to as a *handshake*.

Connectionless communication is similar to sending a piece of stamped mail (with no upgrade options) through the regular post office. One does not know exactly when the mail will arrive, nor does one receive any acknowledgement that it was received. This type of connection is used in LANs through the user datagram protocol (UDP) for sending streaming audio or video messages.

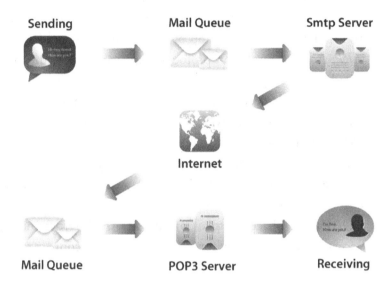

Figure 4.10. Connectionless communication

Below are descriptions of networking protocols used in networks today.

- o *IP*: The most widely used protocol is the internet protocol. It handles all network addressing in a TCP/IP network. IP provides connectionless service for fast but unreliable communication between computers. IP is discussed further in the section below this bulleted list.
- o *TCP*: Transmission control protocol is the primary transport layer protocol.
- o *FTP*: File transfer protocol provides a method for transferring files between computers.

o *Telnet*: An internet protocol that allows you to connect your PC as a remote workstation to a host computer anywhere in the world and use that computer as if it were local. Telnet allows terminal emulation, which is the ability to access a remote computer and use its resources.

o *SMTP*: Simple mail transfer protocol is a TCP/IP protocol used in the process of sending and receiving emails.

o *UDP*: User datagram protocol provides a connectionless transportation service on top of the internet protocol (IP).

o *ARP*: Address resolution protocol maps hardware addresses to IP addresses for delivery of data on a local area network.

o *SNMP*: Simple network management protocol allows network administrators to connect to and manage network devices.

o *PPP*: Point-to-point protocol provides dial-up networked connection to networks. PPP is commonly used by internet service providers (ISPs) as the dial-up protocol for connecting customers to their networks.

o *POP3* (post office protocol 3) and *IMAP* (internet message access protocol) are ways for client computers to connect to mail servers and collect email.

The IP Language

Just as we need a common language with which to communicate with one another, computers in a network environment need and have a language of communication. It is the IP—the internet protocol. M. J. Norton, in *IP as a Second Language*, refers to IP as the universal language of networking. The IP is the most popular nonproprietary protocol suite because it can be used to communicate across any set of interconnected networks and is well suited for LAN and WAN communications.

The internet protocols consist of a suite of communication protocols. The two best known are the transmission control protocol (TCP) and the internet protocol (IP). The internet protocol suite is used for common applications, such as email, terminal emulation, and file transfer. This section discusses the IP suite because it is the most used protocol in networking.

Since their early development in the 1960s, the internet protocols have become the foundation on which the internet and the web are based. You will find IP addresses in every network device no matter the size or type of network, be it a home, a company LAN, or the internet. In order for one computer to connect to another, both require an IP address.

Types of IP Addresses

There are two basic types of IP addresses: static and dynamic.

A static IP address is a number that is permanently assigned to a specific computer and does not change. Once a computer has been assigned its IP address, it will keep it indefinitely. The advantage of a static IP address is that the computer will always have the same IP address on the network and will be easy to identify in the future once its IP address is known.

A dynamic IP address is a number that is assigned to different computers at different times. This means that every time a computer is connected to a network, it is assigned a random IP address from a pool of IP addresses, depending on IP availability. For example, if your company network uses dynamic IP addresses, it means that each time you connect your computer to the network, it is given a new IP address.

What We Learned

- The OSI model is a definition of network communication as a series of layers. It describes how network layers interact with one another. There are seven layers in the OSI model:

application, presentation, session, transport, network, data link, and physical.

- A client is a computer or application that receives information or resources from another computer, typically known as a server.
- The server is a program or computer system that responds to and fulfills requests from client computers in a networked environment.
- Two categories of networks are peer-to-peer networks and server-based networks.
- The two main types of networks are local area network (LAN) and wide area network (WAN). A local area network is a computer network covering a small geographic area, such as a home, or one location, such as an office or school, while wide area networks cover geographically separated areas. Network protocols are sets of rules that manage network communications between computers.
- The internet protocol is the most popular nonproprietary protocol suite. It is used for communications among any set of interconnected networks and is appropriate for LAN and WAN communications.

CHAPTER 5

OPERATING SYSTEM FUNDAMENTALS

In This Chapter

- overview of operating systems
- capabilities of the operating system
- server, desktop, and mobile operating systems
- skill sets required for operating system administrators
- how to read candidate résumés and certifications

In this chapter, the topic of the computer operating system is introduced and then expanded upon with details about the types and uses of each operating system. A good understanding of the different operating systems and their uses will help a technical recruiter identify candidates who support and maintain those systems.

It is easy for individuals to copy other people's résumés by swapping the contact details and company names of the original résumé owner with theirs. Thus, it's imperative for a technical recruiter to understand each candidate's experience and skills through a conversation. It's no longer adequate to weigh the number of times a keyword appears on a résumé or approve a candidate as suitable because all the keywords in a job description are found on the candidate's résumé.

What Is an Operating System?

An operating system (O/S) is a program that controls the resources on a computer system. The O/S also controls how other software and hardware on the computer operate. It is used to manage all the computer's resources. For instance, the O/S manages the input and output resources, memory allocation, job scheduling, system boot, and recovery. Every computing device uses an operating system.

The O/S is the first program loaded on a computer system. It provides an interface among the computer's hardware, software, and the user. Figure 5.1 illustrates how the hardware interfaces with the operating system, the operating system with the application, and then the application with the user.

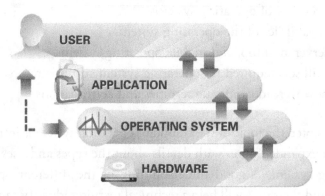

Figure 5.1. Operating system interface with hardware, software, and user

In the simplest terms, the operating system is the middleman between your computer's hardware and yourself. This includes internal and external hardware such as memory, a hard drive, a mouse, and a keyboard. Not so long ago, in the mid-1990s, there were operating systems that were not network capable. Today, almost every commercial operating system is capable of connecting to local and wireless networks. Figure 5.2 further illustrates how the operating system is the center of attention for every software or hardware device installed or connected to the O/S.

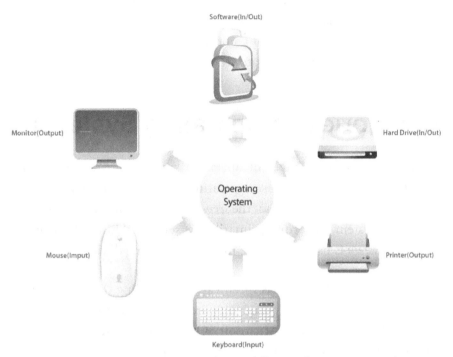

Figure 5.2. Operating system as the middleman between input/output hardware and software

Capabilities of the Operating System

The O/S has many capabilities. Among these, we will focus on three. The first is its ability to *multitask*. The second is its ability to provide *networking* between computing devices. The third is its ability to *secure* the contents of the hosting computer. The O/S performs other tasks too, such as the management of processors, memory, devices, and storage.

- *Multitasking* is a method by which operating systems handle multiple tasks from the same or multiple software applications.
- *Networking* is the ability of an operating system on one computer to connect to another in order to share resources or respond to requests made by the other computer.
- *Security* is the ability of an operating system to protect its host computer from deliberate attacks.

Categories of Operating Systems

There are three main types of operating systems. First, the *desktop operating system* is a single-user operating system that runs primarily on desktop computers. Second, the *server operating system* is a multiuser operating system that runs primarily on servers. Third, the *mobile operating system* is used to operate mobile computing devices.

Each software application has specifications regarding the type of O/S that supports its functions. Some software applications are designed for specific O/Ss. For example, Microsoft SQL Server and Microsoft Access run only on Microsoft Windows O/S. Given that a server O/S affords superior capacity and processing power, applications that require such capabilities must run only on a server O/S. The everyday user may not need a server O/S.

Table 5.1 lists some examples of server applications and their operating system requirements. As shown, Microsoft Exchange Server (Microsoft's email and collaboration software) runs only on the Windows Server O/S and does not work with UNIX or Linux (at least at the time of this writing). The latest version of Microsoft SQL Server (SQL Server 2017 at the time of this writing) can now be installed on both Windows and Linux O/Ss. (SQL Server previously worked only on Windows O/S.) Oracle Database Server works on both Windows and UNIX/Linux O/Ss.

Server Applications	Windows	Linux	UNIX
Microsoft Exchange Server	✓		
Microsoft SQL Server	✓	✓	
Oracle Database Server	✓	✓	✓

Table 5.1. Server applications and the server O/Ss they work with

Closed-Source or Open-Source

Another factor that differentiates operating systems is whether they are open-source, closed-source, or a combination of both (mixed). *Open-source* is a term used to describe whether the operating system is open and available for the public to download, modify, and use without paying for it. In other words, it is free. When a program is open-source, it means that the source code is available for anyone to view or download, whereas *closed-source* suggests that the software is proprietary, and the source code is not publicly available. In other words, one needs to purchase a license to use closed-source software. *Mixed-source* describes when some parts of the software are free but other parts are proprietary.

Desktop Operating Systems

A desktop operating system is an operating system found on client or end user computers. When a computer on a network has a server that controls its access to network resources and security, that server is loosely known as the domain controller. The domain controller controls how and if a desktop computer joins the network, prints, browses the internet, and shares other network resources.

A desktop O/S does not have as much processing power as server operating systems. However, when a desktop is on a network without a domain controller, the desktop is the master of its domain, controlling access to all available resources.

Examples of desktop operating systems are Windows 8, Windows 10, and macOS.

Mobile Operating Systems

A mobile O/S is an operating system used in mobile devices such as phones, tablets, and smartwatches. Mobile O/Ss have special utilities that allow mobile devices to function in a way that was previously distinct from desktops by including features such as a global positioning system (GPS), a touchscreen, Bluetooth, a cellular phone, camera, speech recognition, and so on. You might argue that today's desktop O/Ss offer all these features too, and you would be correct. These days, there are very few features that differentiate their functionalities, except that one is a mobile handheld device, and the other is not.

Examples of mobile operating systems are Android, iOS, Google Pixel UI, and Windows 10 Mobile.

Server Operating Systems

A server O/S is an operating system installed on a computer identified as a server in a client-server network environment. It controls the network, the resources on the network, and desktop computers attached to the same network as the server computer. A server O/S communicates through LANs and WANs to allow users to share files, disks, printers, and other network resources.

A server O/S provides data integrity and security by allowing and restricting access to certain resources and files. It utilizes administrative tools for adding, changing, and removing users, computers, and peripherals from the network. In addition, the server O/S has troubleshooting tools that inform network administrators of network activities. The server O/S includes internetworking support that ties multiple networks together and provides file and print sharing, user account administration, and network security.

Examples of server operating systems are Microsoft Windows Server, SUSE Linux Enterprise Server, macOS Server, HP UNIX, Red Hat Enterprise Linux, and Ubuntu Server.

Operating System Types

You can probably tell the type of network your client has by looking at a job requisition. If the job description is requesting Linux or UNIX skills, then the client is a UNIX/Linux shop. The same is true for Windows. That's as simple as it gets. Now, there are also environments that are combined—where the environment runs both the Windows and UNIX/Linux operating systems based on the software application needs of the organization and the perceived strengths of each operating system.

The manufacturers of the server operating systems listed in table 5.2 compete for the same organizations and thus include mostly the same functionalities for networking, security, file sharing, and disk and storage management. Operating systems fall under UNIX, Linux, Windows, Macintosh, and Mainframe categories. Table 5.2 lists some of the major server operating systems, their manufacturers, and whether they are closed- or open-source.

Name	Manufacturer	Family	Source
AIX	IBM	UNIX	Closed-source
HP-UX	Hewlett-Packard	UNIX	Closed-source
macOS Server	Apple Inc.	Macintosh	Closed-source
Oracle Solaris	Oracle	UNIX	Mixed-source
Windows Server	Microsoft	Windows	Closed-source
z/OS	IBM	Mainframe	Closed-source

| Red Hat Linux | Red Hat | Linux | Open-source |
| SUSE Linux | SUSE | Linux | Open-source |

Table 5.2. Server operating systems

UNIX

Each operating system has its strengths. The general view about UNIX is that it is relatively stronger in its ability to remain uncompromised by viruses, hacking, and security breaches. This is the reason some organizations that implement the Windows operating system continue to utilize UNIX or Linux as the operating system installed on their firewall server. There are many flavors of the UNIX operating system, and the following section reviews the IBM AIX, HP-UX, and Sun Solaris flavors, as well as the macOS Server.

IBM's AIX: IBM's UNIX-based operating system includes functionalities such as system management, security, availability, and virtualization. This operating system supports 32- and 64-bit applications. AIX operates only on IBM hardware systems—IBM UNIX operating system-based servers. AIX provides a system management interface tool (SMIT) referred to as "smitty," used for system administration.

HP-UX: HP's 64-bit UNIX-based operating system's functions include virtualization, system management, security management, clustering, file system management, developers' tools, and partitioning. Because the HP Company is a software company as well as a hardware manufacturing company, the HP-UX operating system operates only on HP hardware servers; the marketing plan is for organizations to purchase both the operating system and server hardware. HP-UX provides its system administration manager (SAM) as a tool used for system administration.

Oracle Solaris: Originally created by Sun Microsystems and purchased by Oracle, its latest release at the time of this writing is the Oracle Solaris

10, with features that include security, performance, networking, data management, interoperability, virtualization, availability, and platform choice (the ability to select server hardware of choice for installation). The Oracle Solaris UNIX-based operating system can be installed on other manufacturers' server hardware, such as Dell.

MacOS Server: Created by Apple Computers, the macOS Server is a Macintosh system that originated partly from the UNIX operating system. It looks similar to MAC desktops in its simplicity but has more operating power since it's obviously a server operating system. The macOS Server comes bundled with server applications such as email, collaboration, calendaring, and chat applications. Just like other Apple products, the macOS Server delivers rich graphics.

Linux

The Linux operating system is increasing in popularity, and Linux is becoming available on many server platforms. Both Red Hat and Novell SUSE Linux are platform insensitive. This means that they can run on as many hardware server computers as possible, from Dell, IBM, and HP to even high-powered personal computers. The ability of the Linux operating system to run on inexpensive hardware and the large number of developers involved in the development of Linux are increasing the widespread use of Linux as the development platform of choice for new business applications.

Red Hat Linux: Created by the Red Hat company, this operating system comes in both server and desktop versions. It is not hardware specific and is also available for mainframe computers. Reasons why organizations both big and small are turning to Red Hat and other Linux-based operating systems include reduced total cost of ownership, the availability of thousands of certified software applications that run on this O/S, open-source technologies, and interoperability with other Unix software.

Novell SUSE Linux: Owned by Novell and similar to Red Hat, Novell SUSE Linux is not hardware specific and is available in both server and desktop versions. SUSE includes functionality such as virtual machine management tools and support for .NET applications on Linux. Many software application companies are getting their software certified as Certified Software Applications on SUSE Linux.

Windows

Windows was created by Microsoft and is available in both desktop and server versions. There is another category of the Windows server, referred to as the Windows Small Business Server (SBS), that comes bundled with Exchange Server for email, SharePoint Services for collaboration, and SQL Server for database. The Windows SBS is used in small organizations with a maximum of seventy-five users. Similar to other server operating systems, the functionalities of the Windows Server operating system include system management, active directory management, virtualization, web server, networking security, and storage management.

Mainframe

In *Introduction to the New Mainframe: z/OS Basics* by IBM Redbooks, it's noted that a mainframe is the central data repository in a corporation's data-processing center, linked to users through less powerful devices such as workstations or terminals. The presence of a mainframe often implies a centralized form of computing, as opposed to a distributed form of computing. You may wonder why mainframe technology attracts very little attention, even in the IT field. John Kettner, one of the coauthors of this book, wrote in August 2009: "That this is so is perhaps not surprising. After all, who among us needs direct access to a mainframe? And, if we did, where would we find one to access?"

Mainframes tend to be hidden from the public eye and are highly resistant to most forms of abuse that badly affect personal computers, such as email-borne viruses and Trojan horses.

IBM z/OS: The z/OS mainframe operating system is manufactured by IBM, and its latest release is Version 1 Release 11. It's the most widely used and advertised mainframe operating system from IBM. It functions as a central repository to keep applications and data available and secure.

Operating System Skill Sets

As a technical recruiter, one should be cognizant of the fact that just because a candidate has had the opportunity to work in a high-profile network environment and has become familiar with the environment does not mean the candidate has the required skill sets or that the candidate implemented or supported the network.

When recruiting operating system administrators, recruiters need to understand how an operating system skill set supports an organization's IT infrastructure. The most common operating systems are mainframes, UNIX, Linux, and Windows. In the following section, we cover the most common skill sets sought after for managing and supporting each operating system.

Windows Skill Sets

The skill sets you see in a Windows administrator candidate résumé or job description requirement include managing the hardware and software components, the users in the network, the security, and the file system. Every Windows administrator must have good skills in these areas and should be able to answer questions on how he or she configures and performs troubleshooting activities on these tools. We discuss the questions to ask candidates in a later section.

Résumé Phrases, Windows System Administrator

Active directory administration, domain trusts administration, DHCP, DNS, organizational units (OUs), TCP/IP, OSI Model, group policy, LAN security, IIS, WINS, SMTP.

Figure 5.3. Phrases on a Windows system administrator's résumé

Active directory (AD): The directory service stores information about objects on a network and makes this information available to users and network administrators. AD gives network users access to permitted resources anywhere on the network using a single log-on process. It provides network administrators with an intuitive, hierarchical view of the network and a single point of administration for all network objects. Active Directory Users and Computers is an administrative tool used in performing the day-to-day administrative tasks of managing network users, their computers, security, and user access to resources. The Windows system administrator should know how to use AD to create, delete, modify, move, and set permissions on objects stored in the directory. The Windows systems administrator should also have experience creating and configuring AD objects such as organizational units (OUs), users, contacts, groups, computers, printers, and shared file objects.

Internet Information Server (IIS): A software service that supports website creation, configuration, and management along with other internet functions. Internet Information Server includes network news transfer protocol (NNTP), file transfer protocol (FTP), and simple mail transfer protocol (SMTP). IIS has many tentacles. With the advancement of web-based programming, software manufacturers are creating web-based counterparts of their applications, and as a result, IIS, with its web configuration function, is utilized in most web-enabled applications created by Microsoft. Applications like Microsoft SQL Server Reporting

Services, Dynamics Customer Relationship Management, FTP, SMTP, and WWW publishing are all examples of tools that require IIS to function. This makes IIS an important tool for every Windows system administrator to understand and to be able to configure and manage.

Simple mail transfer protocol (SMTP): SMTP is a member of the TCP/IP suite of protocols that governs the exchange of email between message transfer agents. It transports email through a network. A Windows administrator worth his or her pay should know the inner workings of this protocol and how to configure it in a network environment.

Dynamic host configuration protocol (DHCP): This is a TCP/IP protocol that dynamically leases IP addresses to network client computers. DHCP uses a client/server model where the DHCP server maintains centralized management of the IP addresses that are used on the network. DHCP prevents IP address conflicts (where two client computers have the same IP address). The Windows systems administrator needs solid experience in configuration and administration of DHCP clients and servers in a network.

Domain: A domain is a group of computers that are part of a network and share a common directory database. A domain is administered as a unit controlled by common rules and procedures. A domain provides access to the centralized user accounts and group accounts maintained by the domain administrator. The Windows systems administrator needs to be able to manage multiple domains, domain trust relationships, and security.

Virtual private network (VPN): VPN connections are extensions of a private network that include encapsulated, encrypted, and authenticated links across shared or public networks. VPN connections provide remote access and routed connections to private networks over the internet. The Windows systems administrator must have experience in administering VPN connections for end users and also managing appropriate VPN security.

UNIX/Linux Skill Sets

The skill sets you see on a UNIX/Linux administrator résumé or in a job description requirement include the components of the operating systems that help in the administration of the users in its network as well as the management of hardware and software components, security, and the file system. Aside from being able to answer questions on how he or she configured and performed troubleshooting activities, every UNIX/Linux administrator must be skilled with the ability to use most UNIX commands and utilities. Those utilities are listed in figure 5.4.

Résumé Phrases, UNIX System Administrator

UNIX/Linux, Red Hat Enterprise Linux, Perl, C++, RCS, CVS, Postfix, QMail, Sendmail, procmail, CGI, Shell Scripting, SSH, Kerberos, DNS, NFS, SMTP, DHCP, Samba, NetBSD, FreeBSD, PGP, GPG, and X Window System.

Figure 5.4. Phrases on a UNIX system administrator's résumé

Programming/scripting: Scripts are used for performing administrative tasks. Administrators can write scripts that automate these tasks, making the daily and monthly tasks as simple as a click of a button. The UNIX/Linux administrator should know how to write scripts using Perl5, Shell Scripting, and Vi Editor.

Software configuration and administration: There is a lot of software available in the UNIX environment, some of which is used for web server, directory, mail system, and domain service administration, to name a few. The list of software tools includes Apache HTTP/HTTPS Servers, DNS, NFS, NIS/YP, POP, IMAP, IMAPS, SMTP, Postfix, QMail, Sendmail, procmail, listserv, mhonarc, PPP, FreeBSD, source code control (CVS, RCS, SCCS), and X Window System. The UNIX/Linux administrator should be familiar with most of the listed software that run in this environment; this administrator should also know how to use these tools to manage users, security, file systems, network resources, network access, mail systems, and optimizations.

Security: Being able to secure the UNIX operating system is an important skill that all O/S administrators must have. In UNIX, the knowledge of UNIX security, firewall setup, and configuration with Juniper Netscreen and IPFilter are crucial. Local and wide area network security as well as VPN security are also skills the administrator should have. The following are complementary security components the administrator should know: IPSEC, encryption (PGP, GnuPG, SSL), SSH, Kerberos, security policy planning, and network security auditing.

Networking: The candidate must have a practical understanding of the network protocols, such as TCP/IP, UDP, ICMP, and so on. The UNIX/Linux administrator should know how to use simple connection commands such as telnet (a program that lets you log in to use other computers on a network as if you were sitting in front of the other computer). In addition to protocols, the UNIX administrator should have network troubleshooting and maintenance skills, including configuring network utilities such as DHCP, SNMP, IPv6, HTTP (hypertext transfer protocol), POP3 (post office protocol), IMAP (internet message access protocol), SMTP (simple mail transfer protocol), DNS (domain name service), LDAP (lightweight directory access protocol), and NFS (network file system).

Mainframe Skill Sets

Mainframe system administrators perform the day-to-day tasks of maintaining business data that reside on the mainframe as well as maintaining the system itself. Mainframe system administrators have specializations that include database administrator (DBA) and security administrator. Mainframe system administrators are very interested in how end user applications are utilized; therefore, they have more interactions with end users than their counterparts in UNIX and Windows environments. Mainframe system administrators oftentimes interface directly with the application programmers and end users to make sure that the administrative aspects of the applications are met. Consequently, the system administrator role is key to the smooth operation of a mainframe system. We have identified some skill sets required for the mainframe administrator, including the following.

TSO/E: Time Sharing Option/Extensions (TSO/E) allows users to log on to z/OS and use a set of basic commands. It provides a log-on capability and a command prompt interface to z/OS. Most administrators work with TSO through its menu-driven interface and Interactive System Productivity Facility (ISPF). It's a given that the mainframe system administrator has the skills to use TSO/E to configure multilevel security that creates an environment that requires security label at log-on.

ISPF: Interactive System Productivity Facility provides a menu system for accessing commonly used z/OS functions. ISPF provides utilities, editor, and ISPF applications to the administrator to use in developing interactive applications. The system administrator has access to almost all z/OS system functions using the ISPF and thus needs to know how to manage the ISPF environment.

z/OS UNIX shell and utilities: The z/OS UNIX shell and utilities provide an interactive interface to z/OS, allowing administrators not only to write and invoke shell scripts and utilities but also to use the shell programming language. Shell scripts are a list of shell commands created with the shell programming language. Since IBM mainframe systems now include UNIX tools and utilities, the mainframe system administrator is expected to know how to use UNIX commands to perform administrative tasks in the z/OS environment.

Data management in z/OS: Data management involves all the system administrative tasks of data allocation, placement, monitoring, migration, backup, recall, recovery, and deletion. Storage management can be done either manually or through automated processes. The system administrator should know how to use the Data Facility System

Managed Storage (DFSMS) utility to automate storage management for data sets.

Batch processing and the job entry subsystem (JES): Much of the work running on z/OS consists of programs called batch jobs. Job entry subsystem (JES) manages the flow of batch jobs in a z/OS system. Batch processing is used for programs that can be executed with minimal human interaction and at a scheduled time or on an as-needed basis. The system administrator should know how to use JES to manage data input and output as well as job queues.

Workload Manager (WLM): This is a component in z/OS that manages the processing of workload in the system according to the company's business goals. It is a required skill for the mainframe system administrator.

Job Control Language (JCL): JCL tells the system what program to execute and provides a description of program inputs and outputs. The system administrator is expected to know how to use this tool to set up and administer batch jobs.

Customer Information Control System (CICS): CICS enables the availability of legacy system applications on the internet. The system administrator should be able to use CICS programming commands for transactional subsystems of z/OS that run online applications.

Resource Access Control Facility (RACF): Used for securing the z/OS system, the RACF provides the basic security framework on a z/OS mainframe. The mainframe system administrator should know how to set up this framework for the purposes of identifying and authenticating users, authorizing users to access protected resources, and the logging and auditing of attempted unauthorized access.

Résumé Phrases, Mainframe System Administrator

ISPF, TSO/E, JCL, z/OS administration, CICS, WLM administration, system administration using z/OS UNIX Shell and utilities, knowledge of the main components of the IBM Mainframe z/OS architecture—DFSMS, RACF, TSO, ISPF, JCL, batch processing and scheduling, and JES.

Figure 5.5. Terms on a mainframe system administrator's résumé

Figure 5.5 lists portions of the skill terms you typically find in a job description on a résumé for a mainframe system administrator. Having read the explanations above, you will find it easier to understand the acronyms and the skill sets needed.

Conversation between a Technical Recruiter and a System Administrator

There are a number of questions a technical recruiter might ask a system administrator to better understand their focus. Most candidates feel that recruiters do not have much knowledge about the intricacies of their technical skills; that is why we start this recruiter-to-candidate conversation with a tone that makes the candidate feel like they can actually relate to the recruiter.

The recruiter may start by going through the preliminaries of basic recruiter and candidate greetings and then flow right into the interview. Please note that this exchange is based on the Windows system administrator skill sets.

Greeting:
"Hi. My name is Helen Olive from ABC Solutions. I saw your résumé online and wanted to find out more about your skill sets in relation to a position I have today … Is that okay?"

Interview:
"I appreciate your help. I enjoy listening to how system administrators solve business problems. I'm going to ask you some general questions; your answers will give me a better understanding of what you do and perhaps what you enjoy the most in your job."

- "Please describe your networking environment—the platform supported, number of users, and security configuration. Tell me about your team. How many other system administrators do you work with and how are your responsibilities divided?"
- "Of all the network application technologies and protocols you are familiar with, which do you work with on a daily basis? How do you use them?"
- "You listed Active Directory on your skills profile; please tell me how this is configured in your company. Did you inherit this configuration, or were you part of the original AD planning?"
- "From your experience with Active Directory, please tell me some of the considerations you have for designing, configuring, or managing your Active Directory environment."

The subjects of these questions can be substituted to match any of the skills being recruited for. After this conversation, based on the answers received from the candidate, the recruiter can determine whether to move the candidate forward to the next step in their recruiting process.

Desktop versus Network Administration

How does one differentiate between a desktop systems engineer and a network systems engineer, both of whom are certified? Certification descriptions have changed for the better, making it easier to distinguish between the levels of expertise of an expert and an entry-level specialist. For example, a Microsoft Certified Solutions Expert (MCSE) is an expert, while the Microsoft Certified Solution Associate (MCSA) is an entry-level specialist.

A network engineer or administrator is usually seen as more senior and experienced than a desktop administrator. The network engineer usually progresses to this position from desktop administration. The desktop engineer/administrator, for the most part, has direct communications with the end user, providing support and configuring the operating systems, applications, and network access on desktop computers. The network engineer's contact with the end user is through the desktop engineer; the network engineer designs, implements, and manages the physical and logical network infrastructure, which may include router, switch, storage, and data center configurations.

In figures 5.6 and 5.7 are job description samples of the desktop systems and network systems administrator/engineer roles. This section will examine both roles to find out the differences and similarities between desktop- and network-focused administrators.

SAMPLE

MCSE Desktop-System Engineer Job Description Sample
Skills: MCSA, Windows Server 2012, active directory, server, exchange server, MS Office 365, TCP/IP, routing, troubleshooting, Symantec Ghost, McAfee, HP MSA SAN.
- Thorough understanding and demonstrated experience in TCP/IP, DNS, DHCP, EIGRP, OSPF, and BGP routing protocols.
- Experience with various business-class and consumer-class WAN transports, including DS3, T1, cable modem, DSL, wireless, and microwave.
- Good knowledge of various internetworking concepts, such as SNMP, PPP, HSRP, NAT, IPSec, CEF, Ether Channel, bonding, load balancing, and ATM.
- Solid knowledge in LAN, WAN, MAN, VPN, and network security technologies.

Figure 5.6. Sample job description of a desktop engineer

SAMPLE

MCSE Network Engineer Job Description Sample
Skills: MCSE, CCNA, network architecture, RAID, SAN technology, infrastructure design, Cisco, Enterprise class network, scripting.
- Design, implement, and maintain servers, switches, and routers.
- Implement high availability environments, including Citrix, SQL Clustering, active directory, and EMC storage subsystems.
- Conduct performance tuning analysis, capacity planning, workload modeling, and forecasting. Experience in crafting standard operating procedures (SOPs) and (or) service-level agreements (SLAs).
- Good knowledge of voice and data networks.

Figure 5.7. Sample job description of a network engineer

The differentiating criteria are usually based on years of experience, technology environment, network storage experience, and network application implementation.

- **Years of experience**: The first impulse might be to immediately use this metric to separate a desktop engineer from his or her network engineer counterpart. However, to the experienced recruiter, this is not usually so. He or she knows that candidates may decide for any number of reasons to stay on in the role of a desktop support person even though they possess the same level of certifications and years of experience as their network engineer counterpart. Though years of experience may be a factor that helps in the determination of whether a person is desktop or network inclined, it helps to use other metrics in conjunction with this factor.

- **Technology environment**: Just like the previous metric, this should also be used in conjunction with others to make a determination. In letting your candidate describe their environment, you as the recruiter are listening for their familiarity and experience in the position being recruited for. Remember that just because a person has worked in a high-profile network environment with extensive configurations of routers and network appliances does not necessarily mean that they were actually part of the implementation or support of the network.

- **Network storage experience**: Implementations of storage access networks (SAN) and network-attached storage (NAS) are also indications of a person's inclination toward being a network engineer. Desktop administrators are more focused on end user activities; since SAN and NAS are far removed from the end user and closer to infrastructure management, they fall into the domain of the network administrator.

- **Network application implementation**: In most cases, whenever you see reference to VPN, McAfee, and Symantec Ghost in a person's résumé, this is usually an indication of their level and type of experience; these are technologies used mostly in desktop environments, thus pointing to the fact that this person may be a desktop support person and not a network engineer.

Network Administrator versus Architect

Another distinction you will find in systems administration is the role difference between a systems administrator and an architect. Advanced systems administrators are sometimes called architects. Architects have a higher-level view of the organization's information systems. They understand how all systems are connected to serve the needs of the organization.

The systems administrator and architect roles may involve similar tasks, but they are different in many ways. The *systems administrator* does the setup, configuration, and maintenance of specific systems and networks. The systems administrator's focus is mostly on the maintenance of specific systems (e.g., UNIX or Windows). The *architect* is a well-rounded individual with working knowledge of not only specific systems but also how all the systems work together to serve the needs of the organization. In other words, the architect has both technical as well as business knowledge. In addition to their training and formal education, architects acquire most of their knowledge from many years of experience. The administrator's knowledge is mostly acquired through training and formal education. What this means is that the architect usually has many more years of experience than the systems administrator. Another factor that separates the architect and system administrator is that architects are sometimes required to have a "systems engineering" background. Systems engineering focuses on the design and management of interrelated systems.

Essentially, the architect is more of a strategic thinker, commands more money, and sometimes doubles as a CIO. This person has more breadth of understanding and knows the importance of business and technology alignment.

The change in title from a systems administrator to architect generally garners an increase in salary of about $20k–$40k. Usually, the title of *architect* is a promotion offered to top-notch systems administrators. As a technical recruiter, you are probably aware of the effect of job titles on remuneration. Table 5.3 displays the differences in salary between the administrator job title and the architect job title.

From:	To:	Salary Increase
Systems administrator	Storage architect	$20–40K
Network administrator	Infrastructure architect	$15–$30K
Database engineer	Data architect	$20–$40K

Table 5.3. Systems administration job roles

Architect Roles In-House

There is great disparity in how the role of an architect is viewed. Some architects are involved in strategy formation and in helping create an overall big picture that shows the interdependencies among all the systems in the organization and their impact on the business, while other architects are involved in the day-to-day tasks of network administration and resource allocation.

What this means is that the role of an architect differs in each organization. While it is generally safe to assume that architects are big picture thinkers, try to also understand the details of what they do. That is, understand the job description.

We discuss four architect roles below: enterprise architect, solution architect, infrastructure architect, and storage architect.

Enterprise Architect

The enterprise architect (EA) works on defining the architecture of an entire organization, including the business, software, infrastructure, and security of that organization. The enterprise architect defines how all these work together in alignment with an organization's business direction.

A typical job description for an enterprise architect includes these directives:

- o Establish a process that is focused on building and maintaining an enterprise and ensuring its alignment to the organization's business needs.
- o Understand business goals and create high-level design to be used and interpreted by network engineers, application designers, and database designers in an enterprise to manage information more effectively. This design must ensure the integration of all the parts of IT in an organization.
- o Facilitate the adaptation or change of technology to the changing business needs of an organization.

Required skills include a wide range of experience in different technologies and their interoperability, including the following:

- o *Operating systems*: Oracle Solaris, Windows Server, HP UNIX, Linux
- o *Database systems*: Oracle Server, SQL Server, Siebel, Teradata
- o *Development tools*: Java, C#, ASP.NET, JavaScript; .NET, J2EE, EJB, Web Services, SOA, design patterns, AJAX, and many more
- o *Other technologies*: Hadoop, HDFS, public cloud, blockchain

Solution Architect

Previously known as an applications development manager, the main role of a solution architect (SA) is to convert business requirements into a design that then forms the basis for a business solution. Through their design, SAs ensure that solutions meet the cost, schedule, scalability, availability, and requirements of the system.

A typical job description includes these points:

- o Understand business requirements and formulate designs, creating a solution structure that meets the various requirements.
- o Communicate the architecture: ensure that everyone involved in the design and implementation of the design understands the architecture.
- o Support the developers: mentor developers while ensuring that they follow the overall architectural design.
- o Verify implementation of the design: ensure that the delivered system is consistent with the agreed architecture and meets requirements.

Requirements include a range of skills for creating blueprints and high-level design diagrams, such as UML (Unified Modeling Language), database design tools, Rational Rose Unified Process, and many more. The position also requires a software engineering background and all the associated software development skills and tool sets, including C#/ Java, API (REST, SOAP), and relational and nonrelational databases (SQL Server, MongoDB).

Infrastructure Architect

Previously known as systems administrator, network engineer, or IT operations manager, the infrastructure architect provides the architecture for any technology that is implemented for the entire organization, as opposed to technology for a specific business group. Typically, the individual in this role architects the infrastructure elements that every business group requires, such as networks, storage, operating systems, security, and messaging. The infrastructure architect also manages servers, middleware, and client systems.

A typical job description might include the following:

- o Develop and maintain the strategy, models, road maps, policies, and procedures for systems management and monitoring, security, capacity planning, storage, operating systems, servers, and networks.

Required skills include network configuration, storage management, performance, scalability configuration, and security engineering.

Storage Architect

The storage architect designs and develops the organization's server storage software. He or she oversees the enterprise administration of all data backup, archival, and recovery processes. Storage architecture is one of the most important aspects of infrastructure and network management. The cost of purchasing and managing storage has grown to be a significant part of any technology group.

A typical job description includes these requirements:
o   Establish guidelines for space management, data backup, retrieval, and recovery.
o   Ensure the security and availability of stored data.
o   Purchase or negotiate contracts with datacenters.
o   Reduce total cost of ownership (TCO) through optimization.

Required skills include the following:
o   Experience configuring data center solutions, cloud, and infrastructure as a service (IaaS).
o   Backup and recovery solutions with EMC Networker and Symantec NetBackup.
o   Storage area network (SAN) storage consolidation and virtualization as well as backup to disk, virtual disk, tape, and virtual tape.
o   Experience with SAN technologies like Fiber Channel and IP-based storage network solutions.

What We Learned

- An operating system is software that controls the resources on a computer system, how other programs or software behave on the system, and the overall management of a computer system's resources.
- The main capabilities of an operating system are its abilities to multitask, to provide networking between the hosting computer and other computers and peripheral devices, and to secure the contents of the hosting computer.
- There are three main types of operating systems. A desktop operating system is a single-user operating system. A mobile operating system is an O/S used on mobile devices such as phones and tablets. A server operating system is a multiuser operating system installed on server computers.
- A desktop operating system is the operating system found on client or end user computers, such as Windows 10. A server operating system is an operating system installed on a computer identified as a server in a client-server network environment. A server operating system controls the network, the resources on the network, and desktop computers attached to the same network as the server computer.
- A network administrator is usually seen as more senior and experienced than a desktop administrator. The network administrator plans, configures, and implements the overall network, including security, access levels, and more. A desktop administrator deals with end users and their desktop operating systems and applications, supporting and troubleshooting issues arising from end users.
- There are differences between the systems administrator role and the architect role. The systems administrator's focus is mostly on the maintenance of specific systems (e.g., UNIX or Windows). The architect has working knowledge of not only specific systems but also how all the systems work together to

serve the needs of the organization. The architect has both technical as well as business knowledge.

- The enterprise architect works on defining the architecture of the whole organization, including the business, software, infrastructure, and security of the organization.
- The solution architect's main role is to convert business requirements into a design that forms the basis of a business solution.
- The infrastructure architect provides the architecture for technologies implemented for the whole organization, as opposed to technology for a specific business group.
- The storage architect designs and develops the organization's server storage software. He or she oversees the enterprise administration of all data backup, archival, and recovery processes.

CHAPTER 6

THE SOFTWARE DEVELOPMENT LIFE CYCLE (SDLC)

In This Chapter

- the SDLC in a nutshell
- phases of the software development life cycle (SDLC)
- job roles found in each phase
- how the SDLC comes together

As a technical recruiter, you may have seen references to the SDLC in almost every software development, quality assurance, business analyst, and project management position. It is because the SDLC is the foundation for successful software development. To start and finish any project that involves other resources, there must be a process in place that defines each person's role, the engagement plan, progress, and the handover process. The SDLC is that process.

The software development life cycle (SDLC) has several phases that mark the progress of systems analysis and design effort. Within this process, a software product follows a life cycle from its creation to its testing to its introduction to the market. The technical recruiter who works with candidates in software development must understand these phases, the relationships between the phases, and the job roles present in each phase.

This chapter provides an overview of all the phases of the SDLC, their deliverables, and the roles and responsibilities of each job title in each phase. The knowledge elaborated in this chapter is key for every technical recruiter looking for talent in any phase of software development. The recruiter must understand who the business analyst (BA) is, why this role is seen in most phases, and why most job requirements for the BA look for business as well as technical and documentation skills.

Reading through this chapter, a technical recruiter will be able to see how the business analyst, as a result of this role's familiarity with all SDLC phases, can become a project manager. The difference between a project manager and a technical project manager is also made clear, along with situations where one may be preferred over the other.

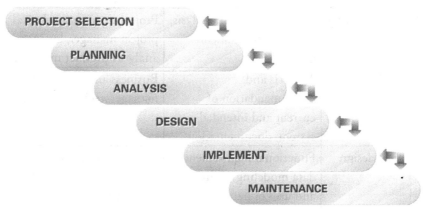

Figure 6.1. The software development life cycle (SDLC)

Looking at Figure 6.1, it may seem as if the steps in the life cycle are sequential, but this is usually not the case. The steps of the sequence are meant to be adapted or used as a guideline for creating any product. Some activities in one phase may be completed in parallel with other activities in another phase. Some phases are iterative, which means that they are repeated until an acceptable system is found. The SDLC pattern used in organizations may differ from one place to another, but many of these steps are still widely applied in software development.

The SDLC in a Nutshell

Table 6.1 shows the stages of the SDLC, their deliverables, and the job roles involved in each stage.

Stage	Deliverables	Job Roles
Project initiation and selection	Project approval, architecture of data, network, software	Management, data architect, software architect, enterprise architect, business analyst / product manager
Project planning	Business and cost analysis, business requirements gathering	Project manager, technical project manager, business analyst / product manager
Analysis	Analysis and recommendation of current and intended system, documentation	Business analyst / product manager, technical writer
Logical design	Functional requirement, data modeling, sources and uses of data or resources, documentation	Data architect, software architect, business analyst / product manager, technical writer

Physical design	Technical functional specification	Infrastructure architect, operations, business analyst / product manager
Implementation	Coding, testing, training, user acceptance testing, installation, configuration management, documentation	Application developer, database developer, quality assurance, tester, business analyst / product manager, DevOps, configuration manager, project manager, system administrator, network engineer, database administrator, technical writer
Maintenance	New product releases, updates, training, support, documentation	System administrator, network engineer, configuration manager, business analyst / product manager, technical writer, trainer

Table 6.1. SDLC snapshot

Of all the deliverables in the SDLC process, the most important is the delivery of software requirements. Software requirements were defined by Sommerville in 1997 as:

> A specification of what should be implemented. They are descriptions of how the system should behave, or of a system property or attribute. They may [also] be a constraint on the development process of the system.

Every project needs to have a software requirement. Frederick Brooks describes the critical role of the requirements process to a software project in his 1987 essay "No Silver Bullet: Essence and Accidents of Software Engineering." He states:

> The hardest single part of building a software system is deciding precisely what to build. No other part of the conceptual work is as difficult as establishing the detailed technical requirements, including all the interfaces to people, to machines and to other software systems. No other part of the work so cripples the resulting systems if done wrong. No other part is more difficult to rectify later.

The three levels of software requirements according to Wiegers's 1999 book, *Software Requirements*, are business requirement, user requirement, and functional requirement, of which business requirement represents the highest level of objectives to an organization. User requirement describes tasks the users of the system must be able to accomplish. These user requirements are captured in use cases, which are scenario-based descriptions of what a user should be able to do with the system. Functional requirement is software functionality that developers must build into the software product to satisfy the business requirement.

The task of creating the software requirements is often performed by the business analyst or product manager. The product manager is the owner of the product in question, creating the product or software system. In some companies, the business analyst is actually the product manager, just with another name.

As you can see from table 6.1, the business analyst / product manager is found in all the phases. An organization may choose to have the business analyst and product manager in all the phases except the logical and physical design, where only the data architect, software architect, and infrastructure architects work to create a technical design based on the business requirements received from the business analyst and product manager.

The Business Analyst and Software Requirements

The business analyst can be found in all phases of the SDLC, sometimes as the main character, other times as just a go-to person who provides feature clarification throughout the development cycle, refining features as necessary. Right from the beginning of the project, the business analyst is the person who either creates the product or, in some cases, is handed the high-level software requirements from the product manager.

Wiegers's *Software Requirements* specifies the following purposes of the software requirement document.

- Customers and the marketing department rely on the software requirement to know what products they can expect to be delivered.
- Project managers base their plans and estimates of schedule, effort, and resources on the product description contained in the software requirement document.
- The software development team relies on the software requirement document to understand what is to be built.
- The testing team uses the product behavior descriptions to derive test plans, cases, and procedures.
- The software maintenance and support staff refer to the software requirement document to understand what each part of the software is supposed to do.
- The training team also uses the software requirement document to help them develop educational materials.

Figure 6.2 displays a sample business analyst's job description in which the responsibilities include creating business requirements and specifications, acting as a liaison between all the groups that will be affected by a new or updated product, and working with software testing teams to create test cases and test scenarios. In short, the business analyst of this job description is seen as the glue that binds all groups together and is the bridge across which all development phases must pass. Being the go-to person for almost every product clarification, the BA is often expected to be a product and business know-it-all. In a later section in this chapter, we discuss the connection between the business analyst and the product manager.

SAMPLE

Overview

The business analyst has the primary responsibility to gather, analyze, validate, specify, verify, and manage the needs of the project stakeholders—clients and business users. The business analyst is part of the technology team and serves as the liaison between the business managers and the software development team. This business analyst is involved at every level of the entire software development life cycle.

Responsibilities

(1) Develops and maintains a thorough understanding of the needs of the group from a business and technical perspective. Works closely with development, quality assurance, systems, and customer care teams as well as clients to capture business requirements and see them through implementation.

(2) Acts as a liaison between the business user and the technical systems groups.

(3) Gathers, analyzes, and documents high-level business requirements. Writes detailed specifications for new or revised systems to ensure that business requirements are met by internal and (or) external resources. Obtains business area sign-off.

(4) Analyzes existing business processes and application functionality. Translates requirements into functional designs.

(5) Runs queries (SQL) to analyze and test data.

(6) Creates test strategies and test cases to ensure quality. Performs integrated system testing and assists with user acceptance testing. Tracks defects and resolution.

(7) Develops project documentation, forms, and training manuals. Conducts training in the business process so that system changes are understood and utilized. Updates system documentation with all system changes made.

Requirements

Bachelor's degree or equivalent business experience

(1) 3+ years of experience in the design and development of complex business systems

(2) experience translating high-level requirements into detailed business requirements and business rules

(3) experience in project management methodologies

(4) thorough knowledge of Microsoft Office applications (Word, Excel, PowerPoint)

(5) experience with software development life cycle (SDLC)

Figure 6.2. Sample business analyst job description

You may have noticed that the business analyst is almost always required to have some technical skills, such as T-SQL (Transact-SQL), used in querying the database. Experience in database reporting tools such as SQL Server Reporting Services (SSRS) and software testing tools also appear as requirements for the business analyst. The business analyst's responsibilities also include analyzing the success of a product launch. The ability to perform this task lies in the analyst's ability to use the technical tools that provide the metrics.

Phases of the SDLC

The phases of the SDLC are project initiation and selection, project planning, analysis, logical and physical design, implementation, and maintenance.

Project Initiation and Selection Phase

This is the first phase of the SDLC. This is where an organization's needs are identified, analyzed, and prioritized. An organization makes a determination after the analysis of its needs whether to dedicate resources to a particular project (new development or enhancement).

Some criteria for selecting one project over others may depend on answers to the following questions.

- Does this project have backing from management?
- Is this the appropriate time for this project?
- Does this project improve the organization's goals?
- Are resources available?
- Is this project worthwhile in comparison to others?

Job roles in the project identification and selection phase are management, architects, and business analysts.

o *Management* analyzes and approves the system.

o *Data, software,* and *enterprise architects* are responsible for making sure the organization's strategic business goals are met through the use of technology. They have a wide scope of experience in business as well as technology. They are responsible for designing and creating strategies for the integration and adaptability of data, software, and network systems to the business.

o The *business analyst* in this phase helps with the feasibility study of the project.

Project Planning Phase

This is the second phase of the SDLC. The initial development team is made up of system analysts, business analysts, and project managers. They develop a baseline of activities required to develop the system. In this phase, the project manager identifies all the activities and resources required to complete the project, coordinating all the activities required from the various groups (users, security, design, development, and network and operations personnel). The documentation for this stage must include the following:

- *Scheduling*: There should be a flexible project schedule created by each group's department with time estimates provided by team members.
- *Deliverables*: There must be a clearly defined project objective.
- *Change management*: The project manager (PM) must document a process for controlling the addition or modification of functional requirements when a project is underway.
- *Budget*: The PM, with assistance from each department head, should produce a baseline budget estimate from each group (development, testing, and network) to ensure adherence to the project's budget.

Job roles in the project planning phase are project managers and technical project managers.

- *Project manager*: The role of the PM is to plan, monitor, and finalize projects according to strict deadlines and within budget. This includes acquiring resources and coordinating the effort of team members and third-party contractors or consultants in order to deliver projects according to plan. The PM also defines the project's objectives and oversees quality control throughout its life cycle.

- *Technical project manager*: The technical project manager has all the skills and experience of the project manager as well as technical abilities. This individual is technically savvy and is usually a former senior software developer who got tired of coding and changed careers to manage people instead. This person understands the intricacies of working with other developers and can make better project time estimations and technical objective definitions.

Analysis Phase

This phase of the SDLC is when the needs of the system user are analyzed and documented in detail. This is where the PM and business analyst (BA) document what the system or software will or will not do in a requirements document. At the end of this phase, there should be a software requirements specification document.

Job roles in the analysis phase are business analysts and technical writer / documentation analysts.

- o *Business analyst*: The BA is a major contributor to the requirements specification deliverable. The BA must understand the business requirements of the organization in order to ensure that there is integration between business and technology. The BA has a handle on the functionalities and benefits of a software product, usually from the end user, revenue generating, and technical perspectives. The BA functions in all the SDLC phases from project initiation to implementation.

- o *Technical writer / documentation analyst*: The technical writer (TW) develops written information about the information systems workflow and process flow. Written output includes a range of documents read by technical and nontechnical personnel in all departments. The TW documents functional specifications of a new or old system—its use, access, and capability—and coordinates and participates in training and user acceptance testing (UAT) exercises.

Design Phase

The design phase can include both the logical and physical design, or they can be separated, depending on the organization. This is when the requirements are converted to a logical and physical design of the system. Data and systems modeling come into play in this stage of the SDLC. For instance, a high-level logical design of a data system may include the flow design of all the sources of business data, the areas of use, and the end result. The physical design stage includes detailed systems modeling and detailed specifications that describe all the moving and static parts of the system and how they should work. This stage includes the selection of the programming language, other software systems, hardware specification, and all aspects of the system design. At the end of this phase, there should be a detailed software design document.

Job roles in the logical design phase include data architect, software architect, and technical writer.

o *Data architect*: In this phase, the data architect designs the relational databases used for processing and also for data storage. This person creates the data models for the identified software applications, bearing in mind all the sources and destinations of data. These models describe the system at conceptual, logical, business, and application levels, using one of many data modeling tools, such as Visio, ERWin, and ER/Studio.

o *Software architect*: In this phase, the software architect works with the database architect to design a system that includes all the functionalities of the application, including its use, capabilities, and access.

o *Technical writer*: The TW in this phase documents the designs from the software and data architects after they have been approved.

Job roles in the physical design phase include the infrastructure architect and operations manager.

o *Infrastructure architect:* The infrastructure architect's role is to develop a high-level design plan for the overall physical and technical IT infrastructure used for the information system. This includes evaluating and selecting all technologies required for the application. The goal is to design a physical infrastructure that maximizes the use of all current technology within the organization while accommodating the demand for future reconfiguration. This high-level design describes all the requirements and resources for security, backup, high-availability, storage, and network infrastructure.

o *Operations manager*: The IT operations manager works with the infrastructure architect to design the physical infrastructure requirements of the new or updated system. He or she usually works within the IT operations department.

Implementation

The implementation phase has two stages: the early and late stages. The early stage consists of coding, testing, and code propagation/deployment to a production environment. The late stage includes documentation, training, and user acceptance.

Early Implementation + DevOps

The developers are provided with the software or system specifications. Using the specifications, the developers then start and complete the code writing process. Between the coding, testing, and deployment is a process that has traditionally been called *code configuration management*. This is a process of tracking and merging code versions, performing code build and code release, and deploying the code to production. This is the traditional SDLC process and involves little or no automation.

With the introduction of the DevOps process and job role, this part of the SDLC has become more efficient and automated. If you recall, the purpose of DevOps (chapter 3) is to accelerate the deployment and delivery of applications and services to clients using automation and streamlined processes. To achieve this, the DevOps engineer collaborates with both application development and IT operations teams to fully automate the build and release management processes.

- *Coding*: Software and database developers write the code to create the application.
- *Testing*: Software testers and quality assurance analysts test the application using test scripts, test conditions, and their associated expected outcomes. They compare test outcomes with actual outcomes. When outcomes differ from the expected outcome, a defect is generated. This sets this stage back to coding.
- *DevOps/Code configuration management (CCM)*: After testing has been completed, the DevOps engineer or configuration manager performs the build and release of the code in the testing and staging environments.
- *Deployment*: The new or updated code is then deployed to the production environment where it is used by its intended users. The DevOps engineer or configuration manager performs the deployment.

Late Implementation

The latter part of the implementation stage includes documentation, training, and user acceptance testing (UAT).

- *Documentation*: The user guide is created by the technical writer.
- *Training*: Training is provided to the users of the system.
- *User acceptance testing (UAT)*: This is testing performed prior to acceptance of transfer of ownership by the client for whom the system was designed and built. In this environment, testing is performed to ensure the system meets all the requirements

specified in either the contract or the user requirements specification.

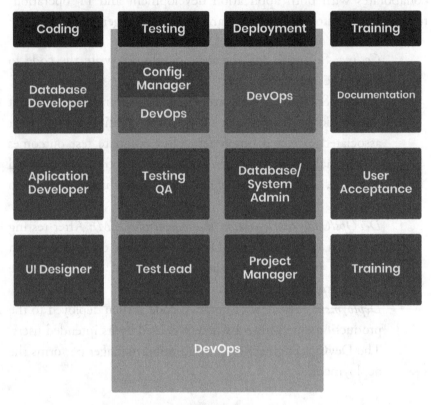

Figure 6.3. SDLC implementation phase

Figure 6.3 displays the job roles in the implementation phase, which include the application developer, database developer, configuration manager, tester / quality assurance, project manager / business analyst, system administrator, database administrator, and network engineer.

In the coding stage, some of the players involved are the database developers, application developers, and user interface designers.

o *Application developer*: Starts coding based on the documented requirements.

o *Database developer*: Starts coding based on the documented requirements.

In the testing stage of a traditional IT environment, you find software testers (quality assurance), business analysts, and a code configuration manager. In a modern IT environment, the DevOps replaces the code configuration manager.

o *Tester / quality assurance:* Plans, designs, and executes effective test cases on a software application to ensure that it functions as designed.

o *Configuration manager:* The configuration manager in this phase moves the code written by developers from the development environment into the quality assurance environment in preparation for software testers to either break or pass the software application. The configuration manager uses version control software like Visual Studio Team Services (VSTS). Each new or updated code is versioned and dated. It is very important for the configuration manager to know which code versions are tested and approved for deployment to the production environment. Systems and database administrators (IT operations) usually assist in the final deployment to production

o *DevOps:* When DevOps processes are available in an organization, they typically replace configuration management. The DevOps engineer automates all the activities previously performed by the configuration manager using specific tools and more efficient processes. These automated processes and tools accelerate the build, release, and deployment processes.

In the deployment stage of a traditional IT environment, you find project managers and IT operations (network engineers, database administrators, and systems administrators). In a modern IT environment, the DevOps engineer works with IT operations, but DevOps is the role that performs code deployment.

o *Project manager / business analyst:* In this phase, the project manager or business analyst acts as a go-to person for the quality assurance analysts and testers, answering questions arising from software functionality tests. He or she also facilitates meetings with all teams to discuss defects, time frame, resources, and go-live planning.

o *System administrator, network engineer, and database administrator:* These participants prepare the production environment and ready it for code propagation. They implement the system, network, and database architecture designs, which includes installing and configuring the prerequisite databases and applications. They also implement the plans for security, backup, high availability, network, and storage. They prepare the entire production environment and get it ready for code deployment. In a traditional IT environment, IT operations deploys code from the staging to the production environment.

o *DevOps:* The DevOps engineer has skills to contribute to both the IT operations (infrastructure) side and the development side. What this means is that DevOps engineers know as much about the production environment (typically an IT operations area and a no-go (prohibited) area for developers) as they do about development. This ensures a smoother, quicker, and error-free deployment.

The last stage is training, which includes documentation, user acceptance testing, and then training. Remember that the roles or tasks in each stage differ for most organizations.

Product Development Landscape

There are usually at least three environments, sometimes four, in most product development landscapes. These are the development, quality assurance, staging, and production environments. When code fails in the quality assurance environment, the phase goes back to development, where the developers fix the identified defect and send it back to the quality assurance environment through the configuration management / DevOps process.

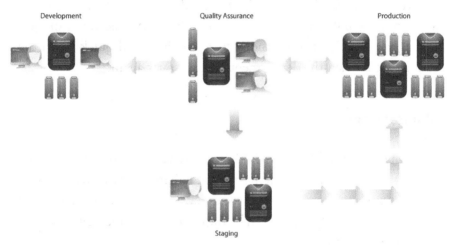

Figure 6.4. Product development landscape

Figure 6.4 illustrates a sample product development landscape. The development team hands off their work to quality assurance (QA). QA tests and does a handover to configuration management / DevOps, who host the product in a staging environment. A staging environment is built as an exact replica of the production environment. The dotted lines from quality assurance to staging and from staging to production show that the staging environment is not always available and can be bypassed. The configuration manager / DevOps performs tests to ensure the effectiveness of the new code in the staging environment. In a traditional IT environment, IT operations (network, systems, and database administrators) will deploy/propagate the tested code to production web servers. In a modern IT environment, deployment is performed by DevOps.

Go-live for web applications requires all hands on deck. The project manager plans out all activities, responsibilities, and the on-call resource list. IT operations prepare the production environment. Next, IT operations / DevOps propagate the tested code to the production environment. IT operations / DevOps monitor performance of the systems once the code has been propagated. Developers are on standby to write quick fixes if the deployed code blows up production. Testers are also on standby to test any quick fixes written. The configuration manager / DevOps is on standby to move the tested quick fix to the staging area. Then the deployment process starts again.

Maintenance

The final stage of the SDLC, the maintenance phase, involves the support of the working system and the enhancement of parts of the system based on users' needs. Once a new system change is requested by customers/users and approved by the organization, the SDLC process starts all over again.

Job roles in the maintenance phase include system administrator, network engineer, technical writer, and trainer.

o *System administrator*: Supports and troubleshoots the software implementation.
o *Network engineer*: Supports and optimizes the hardware, software, and communication links on the software implementation.
o *Documentation/trainer*: Provides end user training and user manuals as well as documentation on the software best practices.

How the SDLC Comes Together

Everything worth doing has to be done well, right? Most things that are done correctly are done with a plan, especially if more than one person is involved. Imagine if members of a development team worked (writing code) without regard for how the code worked with another team's code. It would result in chaos.

The SDLC presents a set of guidelines and processes followed by development teams to create a software product. When properly adopted and implemented, the SDLC ensures that there is a method to the madness involved in software development. Even though there are many phases in the SDLC, each phase can still be broken down into smaller phases. The number of phases adopted by each company depends entirely on its team leaders and software architects.

The combination of phases a company chooses to adopt does not matter. The important thing is that a process was adopted to manage the progress and success of the project.

Sample Software Developed with the SDLC Process

The following scenario is based on an online subscription company of which 75 percent of the revenue is based on member subscription. This organization has a development team that consists of product managers, technical project managers, application developers, database developers, user interface designers, software testers, technical writers, configuration managers, and IT operations (systems administrators and network engineers). Each group has about three to eight persons on each team, including their managers or directors. Business is good, and daily subscriptions are increasing. However, a business must grow by at least 10 percent every year, right? So, the company wants a new product or a product enhancement that will generate more revenue.

TIPS

In some companies, the product manager doubles as the business analyst. Other companies separate the tasks among two or three different people, where the product manager is another name for the business analyst, and the project manager is a separate person.

Stage one: Product managers decide that the quickest way to increase revenue is from the current subscribers. Are there leaks in the system? Are people gaming the system and circumventing subscriptions? Are nonsubscribers getting the benefits of subscription without paying for it? The benefit of subscription is the ability to communicate with fellow subscribers and nonsubscribers. Only paid subscribers are able to communicate. So, the analysis starts and ends quickly with a great find. People were in fact gaming the system.

A new product is born. There needs to be an enhancement product that checks for and stops communications originating from nonsubscribers. Only subscribers can originate email conversations. This analysis uncovered a significant amount of lost revenue based on this problem.

Stage two: The analysis is packaged in a cost-benefit analysis with graphs and presented to stakeholders. Stakeholders deliberate and then initially sign off on this project based on the analysis.

Stage three: Product managers and (or) business analysts and project managers start work performing an in-depth analysis of how the product should work, creating requirement specification documents that contain use case analyses. This document includes process flow information that describes the problems in the system and how they should be fixed. It also includes each use case of the system and what the expected result should be with each case. Software architects, data architects, and operations/infrastructure architects must be part of this stage to ensure that the requirements and the proposed fix fit within the framework of the company. If they find that it does not, they suggest how to adapt or change it.

Stage four: After the document from stage three is complete, the software architects, data architects, quality assurance manager, and IT operations managers are brought in to discuss the new product, its technicalities, and the resources needed from each group. These managers then submit their resource schedules and dates, which are dependent on other project time frames.

Stage five: At this stage, the database developers and application developers start to create the functional requirements. This document describes how the problem in the requirement specification can be fixed at the database and application development level. The developers design all the moving parts of the new system and how they fit within the old one.

Stage six: Development starts and prepares for software testing.

Stage seven: Before testing commences, the configuration manager / DevOps engineer moves the code from the development environment in stage six into the testing environment. Testing can go either of two ways. (1) It can be successful, where there are no defects. Code is then moved to the staging environment and is readied for production. (2) The software testers kick the code back as a result of defects, errors, or misapplied functionality. They may have found a case where a nonsubscriber logs into the website through nonconventional means and is still able to initiate an email, or the testers may have found that subscribers are giving out their email addresses to nonsubscribers, who then communicate with nonsubscribers outside the system. Whatever the case, the developers go back to stage six and then to stage seven again. This iteration may go on a few times before the code is moved to staging.

Stage eight: The configuration manager / DevOps moves the code to the staging environment, where it is ready to be deployed/propagated to the production environment.

Stage nine: In a traditional IT environment, IT operations (consisting of systems and database administrators) deploy/propagate the tested code to production web servers. In a modern environment, deployment is performed by DevOps. The production servers are available to the public. Usually, this initial deployment is performed on only one server. This is because it would be easier to withdraw code from one server if something goes wrong during deployment than from multiple servers.

Stage ten: Complete? No way. The iteration can start all over from stage six again if a problem is found during or shortly after deployment. The software testers start testing the production implementation to confirm that the solution works the same as it would in the real world. After the testing is complete on the one server, then the systems administrators / DevOps propagate the code to all production web servers.

Stage eleven: The technical writer, who has been involved in all the stages, completes the documentation on the product and stores it.

As you can see from this implementation, there was no training involved in this enhancement, yet the SDLC process was followed.

Technical Project Manager versus Project Manager

A project manager's main role is to plan, monitor, and finalize projects according to deadlines and within a specified budget. The main difference between the technical and nontechnical project manager is their background. The technical manager has a technical background, usually a software developer or systems administrator who has led numerous projects in the past and now has a title to go with the work he or she is performing. There are times when there's a need for a technical project manager (TPM) and not the usual project manager—such as when it's necessary for the project manager to understand the need for and apply the full life cycle development in system analysis and design.

When you need a project manager who has had hands-on experience doing the same kind of work that he or she is now asking others to perform, the technical PM can be a better advocate for both sides—the development and the business sides. The TPM is able to communicate to the development team in a language they understand and similarly to the business team. Prior hands-on experience in development projects may enable the TPM to make better time deliverable estimates for the work involved in a development or infrastructure project.

It is worth noting that just because a job requisition requires a TPM does not mean that anyone with a technical background can be presented for the job. When there is a need for a TPM, there is almost always some specific background experience being sought. For instance, when a company is involved with implementing a software development project, the company will look for a TPM with a background in the development technologies currently being used in the company. The same is true when another company is implementing an infrastructure project; the TPM required is usually one with that background. The job and skills requirement in the requisition will usually tell you the background being sought.

Look at table 6.2 to see the similarities and differences between the technical and nontechnical project manager.

Requirements	Technical PM	Nontechnical PM
Background	Must be software development or infrastructure focused	Previous experience in planning and managing large projects; does not need to have a background in technology
Years of experience	7+ years' hands-on experience in a technical capacity	7+ years in planning and managing projects
Education	Bachelor's degree in computer science, business administration, or engineering	Bachelor's degree in business administration
PMP certification	Nice to have but not required and usually not expected	Almost always a requirement
Technical skills	For software development: hands-on skills in SDLC, Windows/UNIX, .NET, Java, SQL Server/Oracle, object-oriented development with Agile, RUP or XP as well as project management tools	Usually SDLC and project management tools

Table 6.2. Technical and nontechnical project manager

Combining the Business Analyst and Project Manager

There are organizations where the business analyst and project manager roles are combined into a single role and called the "product manager." I have worked in such a company. The "product manager" performs the combined role of the BA and PM and is generally defined as a very creative person who defines the road map for a product, creates mockups (prototype/model) to communicate ideas, creates and measures a product's success metrics, and manages the product-building project (project manager), planning and monitoring its execution to meet the deadlines and budget. Figure 6.6 shows a sample of a typical product manager's job description.

SAMPLE

Overview

We're seeking an experienced, creative, high-energy self-starter to join our team. The product manager will own products and features and work closely with the development team, business team, partners, and other divisions to design products that make a difference.

Job Role

- Participate in the development of product road maps.
- Work across functional groups and divisions to gather requirements.
- Define and write product, feature requirements, and functional specifications that articulate current and future business objectives for new products or enhancements to existing products.
- Work closely with technical staff throughout the project life cycle to ensure that interface and technical specifications as well as implementations meet the needs of the product.
- Review milestone releases against product definition, resolving issues affecting expectations and providing direction on definition uncertainties.
- Lead cross-functional teams, including developers, quality assurance, marketing, customer service, and partners to plan and launch projects on time, on budget, and on specification.
- Ensure the quality of the product by working with the quality assurance department to develop use cases, review test cases, and track feature defects.
- Identify necessary reports, metrics, and analysis to measure the effectiveness and success of completed projects.

Requirements

- BA/BS, preferably in technology or business.
- Understanding of software development life cycle.

> - Strong project management skills; organized, attentive to detail, able to manage multiple time-sensitive projects.
> - Demonstrated success managing priorities and personalities in cross-functional teams

Figure 6.6. Typical product manager job description

You may notice that the job description in figure 6.6 is similar to the business analyst job description in figure 6.2. The responsibilities of the business analyst are similar to the product manager, such that they are both required to be liaisons between the development and business teams, to define functional specifications, and to work with quality assurance. However, they differ in two distinct areas. First, the product manager is often required to be a very creative person. Second, he or she is also required to manage the project, thereby acting as a project manager.

What We Learned

- To start and finish any project that involves diverse resources, there must be a plan in place that defines each person's role and includes the engagement plan, progress, and the handover process. The software development life cycle (SDLC) is that plan.
- The SDLC features several phases that mark the progress of systems analysis and design efforts. The technical recruiter who works with candidates in software development must understand these phases, the relationships among the phases, and the job roles in each phase.
- The phases of the SDLC are project initiation and selection, project planning, analysis, logical and physical design, implementation, and maintenance.
  - o The project initiation and selection phase is the first phase of the SDLC; this is where an organization's needs are identified, analyzed, and prioritized.

o The project planning phase is the second phase of the SDLC, where the initial development team that is comprised of the system analysts, business analyst, and project managers develops a baseline of activities required to develop the system. In this phase, the project manager identifies all the activities and resources required to complete the project.

o The analysis phase is where the needs of the system user are analyzed and documented in detail. This is where the project manager and business analyst document what the system or software will or will not do in a requirements document. At the end of this phase, there should be a software requirements specification document.

o The design phase can include both the logical and physical design, or they can be separated, depending on the individual organization. This is when the requirements are converted to a logical and physical design of the system. Data and systems modeling come into play in this stage of the SDLC.

o The implementation phase is where developers start coding. Prior to this phase, the developers would have been handed the design model and the written specification of how the system should be built and how it should work.

o The maintenance phase involves the support and the enhancement of a working system.

CHAPTER 7

SOFTWARE DEVELOPMENT TECHNOLOGIES

In This Chapter

- programming languages
- software developments
- development methodologies
- development frameworks
- software development technologies and how they are used
- job roles in software development
- hiring challenges and staying current with technology

Software development is the process of using a set of tools called a computer language to design a program that runs on a computer to perform or automate a task. A software developer must have the ability to communicate complex ideas and logically break up problems into simple, workable solutions. Another name for software development is programming. A programmer may be very familiar with one or more computer programming languages. The software development skill set is as old as computing itself, and the need for programming skill sets will continue to be as strong as the need to have solutions to problems.

Types of Programming Languages

A programming language is the way in which a programmer instructs a computer to perform functions. There are languages created for the different types of programming, be it writing code that operates devices or writing operating system code. The two basic types of languages are low-level and high-level languages.

Low-Level Languages

The low-level languages are the ones that interface with a microprocessor on a device. They are called "low-level" not because they are unimportant but because of their close proximity to the microprocessor or hardware. Microprocessors interpret instructions in terms of "off" and "on," or "0" and "1." Examples of low-level languages are the assembly and scripting languages.

Assembly Languages

Machine language is considered the native language of CPUs. Given how tedious it is to program in ones (1s) and zeros (0s), almost no one writes programs in machine language. That's why there's an alternative called *assembly language*. In his 2008 book *Beginning Programming for Dummies*, W. Wang notes that the purpose of assembly language is to make programming easier than using machine language. It replaces dozens of error-prone machine language commands with one assembly language command.

One example of assembly language is ARM—Advanced RISC Machine. ARM is an assembly language program that translates the low-level machine language into a quasi-English language known as mnemonics.

Scripting Languages

Scripting languages are considered low-level languages because of their ability to manipulate computer hardware. Wang refers to scripting languages as *system programming languages.* Scripting languages can be used for performing text manipulation, performing systems administration tasks, and automating tasks. Examples of scripting languages are JavaScript, Perl, and VBScript.

High-Level Languages

High-level languages are more intuitive and interpret instructions in almost understandable English. Just as with the low-level languages, the name "high–level" does not mean they are more important than their low-level counterparts. Rather, the name defines their distance from the microprocessor.

However tedious machine language might be, it's the only language processors understand. Even after a program is written in assembly language or a high-level language such as C++, the program still needs to be translated to machine language for the processor to utilize it. This is why there are programs called *assemblers* and *compilers*. The assembler converts assembly language to machine language, while the compiler translates high-level language to machine language.

There are many high-level languages, grouped by how their programming code is structured and organized. A few of these structure groups are object-oriented, aspect-oriented, procedural-oriented, logic-oriented, constraint-oriented, and rule-oriented languages. We discuss object oriented and procedure oriented below. Wang notes that structured programming helps one organize and divide the programs into smaller and more manageable pieces.

Object-oriented programming: The name of this type of programming is derived from how a program is broken down into various components called *objects*. Each object has its own data and functions (types of operations that can be performed on the data). This allows the object to stand on its own as an independent object or be related to other objects where each object can inherit characteristics from other objects.

Examples of the most popular high-level object-oriented programming languages are (1) C# (C Sharp), a .NET programming language used for creating applications; (2) Java, introduced by Sun Microsystems (now owned by Oracle), which is used to create complete applications that run either on a single computer or distributed among servers and clients in a network; and (3) PHP, Hypertext Preprocessor, a language used for creating dynamic web applications.

Procedural-oriented programming: In this type of implementation, programming tasks are broken down into collections of variables and functions that are separate parts of the main program.

Examples of procedural-oriented programming languages are (1) Fortran, used primarily for performing scientific and engineering computing, and (2) COBOL, initially developed as a procedural-oriented language but has recently been revised to also perform object oriented. COBOL's original purpose was for data processing.

Types of Software Development

There are two main areas of programming: applications and systems. Application development uses mainly high-level programming languages to develop applications, while systems development uses low-level programming languages. Application (app) development includes web, desktop, and mobile application development. These three types, plus systems development, are described below. A summary table appears at the end, which you can quickly refer to anytime you need a refresher.

Web Application Development

This is written code that is installed on web platforms and interfaces with users through web browsers like Internet Explorer and Google Chrome. Examples of languages used for web development are C#, VB.NET, HTML, PHP, and Java. Companies are moving toward converting more and more traditional software applications to web applications so that they can be accessed through the internet. For example, Microsoft Office 365 is on the internet (cloud).

Other web-based companies, such as Match.com and Monster.com, have harnessed the power of the internet to create powerful products. These are just two of the popular ones. There are countless other web-based applications from human resources, applicant tracking, and customer relationship management to vendor management applications that are subscription based and generating huge revenues for the owners. The main benefit for the web-based software development company is the dramatically reduced cost of maintenance and support of the software. The software is now maintained at a few servers instead of a thousand different individual installations (as is the case for non-web-based applications). Another advantage for the web-based product is the elimination of piracy. Since the software is web based, there are no copies for software pirates to distribute.

Desktop Application Development

This generally refers to software that is not web based. This type of software is developed for internal use by a company or individuals. Some languages used for nonweb applications are Visual Basic, C#, VB.NET, and Java. Examples of non-web-based applications are desktop applications, time-management software, and disk-copying software. To find examples of these applications, just look at the programs installed on your computer.

Given that the programming languages used in both web and desktop development are the same, you will find that candidates with experience in one area can easily transition to the other.

Mobile Application Development

Mobile app development simply means the development of applications for mobile devices (smartphones, tablets, and smartwatches). Given the differences between mobile devices and other types of computing devices, mobile app developers have to pay attention to screen sizes, operation system platforms, and other constraints related to smaller hardware. When we describe application software as being the interface/bridge between the hardware and user, the focus on interface is even more pronounced in mobile app development. That is, user interface design and user experience design (UI/UX) are important considerations for mobile app development. The key aspects in mobile app development are usability (UI/UX-friendly interfaces), reduced keystrokes, and integration with other application services. There are many examples of mobile application programming. Facebook and Uber mobile applications are just two examples.

Systems Development

On a high level, systems development involves creating software that manages hardware. For example, people who develop operating systems like UNIX, Linux, and Windows are known as systems developers. Examples of languages used for this type of development are C++ and C. The main difference between systems and applications development is that application programs are written to provide services to users, while system programs are written for hardware. An example of system programming is code that processes how a computer manages memory and allocates disks. System programs function on the layer between application programs and hardware. Figure 7.1 displays a simple illustration of a computer system's layers.

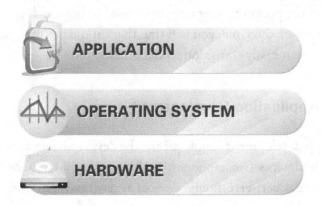

Figure 7.1. System layers

Embedded Systems Development

This is the development of software for microprocessors on devices and objects such as automobiles, cameras, medical equipment, household appliances, vending machines, and toys. Languages used for embedded development are usually referred to as low-level languages. Examples are assembly language and C/C++.

Embedded systems development is very specialized and requires low-level programming language expertise, a thorough understanding of hardware, and an in-depth knowledge of the inner workings of the operating system. Companies that create chip-based products are always in need of embedded systems developers. Figure 7.2 illustrates some examples of embedded system devices.

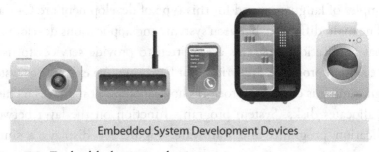

Embedded System Development Devices

Figure 7.2. Embedded system devices

Table 7.1 provides a summary of the main programming languages encountered in job descriptions and on résumés. They are categorized by their level (high, low, or both) and by their primary use for software development.

Language	Level	Software Development
C	Low	Embedded systems
C++	Low	Embedded systems
C#	High	Application (web and desktop)
Java	High	Application (web and desktop)
VB.NET	High	Application (web and desktop)
Objective C	High	Application (mobile)
R	High	Application (web and desktop)
JavaScript	Low and high	Application + embedded systems
VBScript	Low and high	Application + embedded systems
Perl	Low and high	Application + embedded systems
Python	Low and high	Application + embedded systems

Table 7.1. Summary of programming languages

Development Tiers

There is division of labor in software development. Developers get to choose an area of the software on which to focus their skills. These areas are called *development tiers*. You might even have heard them referred to by the name *software architecture*. There are mainly three tiers, or sometimes four, depending on the complexity of the software. The three main tiers are called the *presentation tier, business logic tier,* and *data tier.* Other names for these tiers are *front end, middle layer,* and *back end.* Together, these three tiers are generally called *three-tier architecture.* When there are more than three tiers, it's called *n-tier architecture.* The fourth tier is usually between the business logic tier and the data tier. It is called the *data access tier.* See figure 7.3, which depicts these tiers.

The main reason software has tiers is so that each part can be developed separately from the other parts. Another reason is so that it is easier to maintain. Moreover, each part is developed by people with specialized skills for that tier. Think of a piece of tiered software as your house or apartment. There's the living room, bathroom, bedroom, kitchen, and so on. For efficiency's sake, each room is separated from the others. When the plumbing in the bathroom needs to be fixed, you call a plumber (specialized skill). While the plumber is working on it, the only place that is out of commission is your bathroom and not the whole house (ease of maintenance). Guess what? If your kitchen stove (another part of your house) is also being fixed, you can have both the plumber and stove repair person in the house, working in parallel without getting in each other's way.

A tiered software architecture works almost the exact same way.

- o There's the front-end developer, who works on user interface designs and user experience designs (UX/UI). This person's work is transparent to end users. Information is usually displayed to the user through a browser or client tier.

- o There's also the middle-tier developer, who designs and builds the business logic or business rules that drive business applications (.NET or Java full-stack developer).

- o Then, there's the back-end developer, who designs and builds database objects that allow the business logic to access the underlying data (database developer). This person's work is not transparent to the end user.

Given that software is tiered, specialized developers can work on each part in parallel. When there are issues with the front end, it gets fixed by the front-end developer and does not affect the rest of the application.

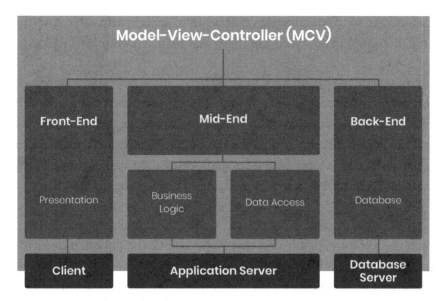

Figure 7.3. Multitier development

In the same way that there are developers who specialize in each tier, there are also software and tools that are used in each tier. Sometimes, you may find a specific software used in more than one tier. Stuff happens. This is similar to when you see a plumber use a hammer. This does not mean that a plumber is a carpenter. It just means that from time to time, the plumber will use a hammer to get the job done, and that's all there is to it.

Hold that thought, because you will use it to be able to tell the difference between specialized developers who happen to have another tier's tool in their toolbox. However, you can still tell what type the developer is by taking a closer look at the full toolbox to see the other tools. If the majority of tools you see are used for a specific tier, then you can make the call.

Let's look at table 7.2 below. I know … it's quite an alphabet soup, isn't it? If you are new to technical recruiting, don't despair. It will only seem like a lot at the beginning. Once you start reviewing those résumés and talking to candidates, you will begin to see why this table (and the alphabet soup) makes your job easier and increases your effectiveness.

I have separated the software tools by tier. This way, you can see which tier uses which specific tools. This will help you when you evaluate a résumé or job description. It will help you answer the question, Is this a front-end, middle-tier, or full-stack developer? "The full-stack developer is usually the developer who does it all." He or she can do some of the front end, the middle tier very well, and a little of the back end.

Getting back to table 7.2, you will notice three major tiers annotated with the job role title for that tier. For example, the presentation tier is usually developed by the front-end and UX/UI developer. The major development technologies are categorized for both Java and .NET frameworks. Also, you might notice that the tools are similar for Java and .NET. This is because most of the tools in this tier are cross-platform (i.e., they work with any framework and operation systems).

Tier / Developer Title	Java	.NET
Presentation layer/ • front-end developer • UX/UI developer	AngularJS, React, JavaScript, API, CSS, XSL, HTML, HTML5, DHTML, AJAX, SPA, TypeScript, jQuery	AngularJS, React, JavaScript, API, CSS, XSL, HTML, HTML 5, DHTML, AJAX, SPA, TypeScript, jQuery, ASP.NET, Winforms, WPF
Business logic layer/ • .NET developer • Java developer	Language: Java Application Server: WebLogic, Tomcat, Apache Web Server	Language: C#, VB.NET Application Server: Internet Information Server (IIS)
Data Access Layer/ • developer	Hibernate ORM, Java Persistence API (JPA), JDBC	LINQ, ADO.NET, nHibernate ORM, Entity Framework

Database layer/ • database developer	Oracle Database, IBM DB2, MySQL, MS SQL Server, TSQL, SQL, PL/SQL, Cloud	MS SQL Server, TSQL, SQL

Table 7.2. Development technologies by tier and programming language

Table 7.3 lists other technologies you will find in software developer positions that will help you decipher the developer type and the environments in which they work. For example, the integrated development environments (IDEs) for .NET and Java are different, and so are the frameworks and data access tools. Another tool you will often encounter is the model-view-controller (MVC). MVC is a development architecture pattern that functions as a "referee" that separates presentation (UI) layer development from the middle and database tiers.

Technology	**Java**	**.NET**
IDE	Eclipse, NetBeans, WebSphere	Microsoft Visual Studio
Operating system	Any	Windows Server only
Framework	Java/Java Enterprise Edition (JEE)	.NET Framework, ASP.NET
Unit testing	JUnit	MS Unit Testing
Data access	JDBC	ADO.NET
MVC	Spring, Apache Struts	ASP.NET
Web services	External through REST API and Web services	Integrated in Visual Studio ASP.NET and supports SOAP, Rest API

Table 7.3. Development technologies for Java and .NET environments

Software Development Methodologies

There are many methodologies used for software development, including Agile, Rational Unified Process (RUP), Rapid Application Development (RAD), Iterative, and so on. The one chosen by the development team depends on whether a plan-driven or an agile process is preferred.

A plan-driven methodology is described by Booch and associates in their 2007 book, *Object-Oriented Analysis and Design with Applications*, as one for which the goal is the definition and validation of a predictable, repeatable software development process. The plan-driven methodology is characterized by following prescriptive activities, relying on well-documented processes, focusing on strategy (rather than on tactics), and managing and controlling (following detailed plans with explicit milestones and verification points within the team).

The agile methodology releases the software developers from following strict steps and allows them to concentrate their creative energies on the development project. The agile process is characterized by doing only what is necessary. It places a reliance on the knowledge of the development team rather than on a well-documented process, focuses on tactics rather than on strategy, is iterative and incremental, and is self-organizing as opposed to predetermined (Booch et al. 2007).

The technical recruiter would encounter these terms not necessarily in a candidate's résumé or job description but rather during a discussion centered on the development experience of a candidate or with a hiring manager describing a company's development process.

The development methodology used in an organization really depends on the knowledge of its development team and the phase of the project. Methodologies can move from agile to plan driven and back again in the course of one project. Since processes often evolve, there should be no hard and fast rule applied to choosing a specific methodology. Each methodology has its benefits and can be mixed and matched to suit the project and team.

Unless the recruiter asks, this information does not usually surface. Therefore, the recruiter must ask in order to find the right candidate for the hiring organization. A candidate who is strictly focused on only one methodology may not be well suited for an organization that mixes and matches methodologies during a development phase. See the call notes below for sample questions you may ask to find out more about your candidate.

"How would you describe your development process?"

"Which methodology do you use?"

"Do you find that your team mixes methodologies to suit the project?"

"If you had the final word, which methodology would you choose?"

CALL NOTES "Think of one particular project. What would you say were the benefits of using one methodology over another for this project?"

The next section describes two examples of development methodologies: Agile and Rapid Application Development.

Agile

Agile means "being able to adapt on the fly." This method of software development is based on adapting, evolving, and aligning requirements and solutions during software development to suit customers' needs. The Agile process is iteration based (a successive series of repeatable tasks). Thus, it requires face-to-face collaboration between development teams (as opposed to following strict written documents) to decide on how to follow the next iterative steps.

Rapid Application Development (RAD)

Rapid means fast or speedy. This method of software development requires very little upfront planning and allows for development (coding) to be done in conjunction with whatever minimal planning needs to be done. As a result, software is written very quickly. Like the Agile process, it is based on iteration. However, unlike Agile, it involves the building of prototypes.

The business requirements and design of the system are created during the prototype construction. Prototyping helps end users and developers verify if business requirements are met. If they are met, developers will formalize the design by building a real system. If requirements are not met in the prototype, developers are given time to refine the prototype in iterative steps until a desired model is achieved. This methodology is used mostly in web development.

Development Frameworks

If you have ever used a template in a word processor (e.g., Microsoft Word) or Excel to create a document, then you know how much time it can save the user. That's similar to what is found in development frameworks—application (template) generators that simplify the process of writing code.

Development frameworks started emerging in the late 1990s as tools packaged with preestablished code to help developers jump-start their application development. The tools help developers generate applications by customizing the code that's already available in the framework.

There are two different categories of frameworks: open-source and proprietary (closed-source). Open-source refers to software with source code that is available for anyone to use, copy, and distribute, free of charge. Proprietary software is the opposite. The source code is not available and can only be used and distributed with appropriate paid-for licenses. Three of the most common and frequently used frameworks are the .NET, PHP, and Java development frameworks.

.NET Framework

The .NET Framework is now an open-source framework from Microsoft for building applications. Developers use .NET to build web applications, server applications, smart client applications, and database applications. Some people assume that .NET is only used for creating web-based applications, but it is actually used for building more than just these.

Below are some technologies included in the .NET Framework:
o Windows Workflow Foundation (WF)
o ASP.NET
o ADO.NET
o WinForms
o Windows Presentation Foundation

PHP Development Framework

PHP is open-source (its code base is freely available), thereby encouraging developers to build frameworks of code that give other developers a jump-start to help develop applications quickly. There are many PHP development frameworks. Here are some examples of PHP frameworks available at the time of this book's writing:
o Symfony
o CodeIgniter
o CakePHP
o Zend

Java Development Framework

Java Enterprise Edition (JEE) is a Java platform designed for mainframe-scale computing, typically seen in large enterprises. It is used the same way that the .NET Framework is used, but it is used with the Java computer language.

Development Technologies and Their Uses

It's usually easier to understand what a widget is when you know what the widget does. So, with this in mind, let's take a look at some of the technologies that go into web development, applications development, and database development and what they are used for. A few specific development technologies have been outlined below.

Name	
ADO.Net	Provides data access to relational database objects. It is part of the .NET Framework.
AJAX	Asynchronous JavaScript and XML is a web development technique used for creating interactive web applications.
AngularJS	A JavaScript front-end web framework that addresses HTML limitations. It extends HTML by providing an uninterrupted user experience during dynamic web page views.
API	An application programming interface enables one program to use facilities provided by another, whether by calling that program or by being called by it.
ASP.NET	Active Server Pages .NET is a web framework for building dynamic web applications. It can be used to build websites that are based on HTML5, JavaScript, and CSS.
C#	A Microsoft .NET programming language for building client-side and server-side applications.

CSS	Cascading Style Sheets is a simple mechanism for adding style in web documents—for example, fonts, colors, or spacing.
Django	Django is a web framework for creating data-driven web applications.
Eclipse	Eclipse is an integrated development environment (IDE) that uses Java programming and is for building Java applications.
Entity Framework	Entity framework is an object-relational mapper for ADO.NET.
Hibernate	Object-relational mapping (ORM) that maps Java classes to database tables. It relieves developers from manual object conversion.
Java	Java is a programming language used to creating applications that run either on single computers or computers distributed across servers and clients in a network.
JavaScript	JavaScript is a scripting language for writing programs that perform administrative functions. It is also used for creating front-end and server-side web applications.
jQuery	A front-end JavaScript library for scripting HTML, creating dynamic web pages, applications, and animations.
LINQ	Language-Integrated Query (LINQ) is part of the .NET framework. It allows developers to write SQL queries and extract data from databases.
nHibernate	nHibernate is an object-relational mapper for the .NET Framework. It allows C#/VB.NET objects to map to relational databases.
NetBeans	NetBeans is an integrated development environment (IDE) for Java and is used to build Java applications.
Objective-C	A programming language used to build macOS and iOS for Apple devices and their respective application programming interfaces.
PowerShell	Used for administration, applications, and general scripting. PowerShell is a task automation and configuration management framework from Microsoft consisting of a command-line shell and associated scripting language.

React JS	A front-end JavaScript library for creating user interfaces (UI).
SOA	Service-oriented architecture is a packaged service that allows different applications to share business processes.
SPA	A single-page application is a type of web page designed to dynamically interact with users without loading a new page for each new interaction.
Typescript	A programming language used to create front-end and server-based JavaScript applications.
Visual Studio	Microsoft Visual Studio is an integrated development environment (IDE) from Microsoft for building .NET applications.
WCF Services	Windows Communication Foundation is a framework for building service-oriented applications.
WPF	Windows Presentation Foundation is a program used for creating UI for Windows applications.

Table 7.4. Technologies and their uses

Job Roles in Software Development

We have discussed the types of software development, which include web, applications, systems, and embedded systems development. In this section, we will identify the job role requirements that correspond to the web, applications, and embedded systems development types.

Applications Developer

Web and desktop applications development call for similar skill sets. Recalling the definitions of web and applications development, web development refers to code that is written and installed on web platforms that interface with users through web browsers such as Internet Explorer or Google Chrome. Applications development refers to code that is not web based and does not interface through web browsers but rather is developed for the internal use of an organization. Both web and applications development use nearly the same development tools and frameworks. For instance, the .NET development framework can be used by both the applications developer and the web developer for software development.

Employers are looking for developers to perform development, unit test, and implement and support code. A college degree is always desirable but is usually not a deal breaker.

Core Requirements for .NET
- o   3+ years in ASP.NET, C#, VB.NET
- o   3+ years in XML, Web services
- o   3+ years in HTML/CSS
- o   3+ years in MS SQL Server

Core Requirements for Open Source
- o   3+ years in PHP, MySQL
- o   3+ years in XHTML, JavaScript, CSS

Elective Requirements
- o   AJAX
- o   VB Script
- o   Visual Studio Team Services
- o   Visual Studio

Embedded Systems Developer

There is a strong requirement for formal education for this job role. This may be because the companies are looking for core engineers with electrical, electronics, or computer engineering degrees. The extent of loss incurred in design issues with device development is usually more than its web, mobile, or desktop counterparts. A web application can usually be fixed with a quick propagation of web code. For example, when there is a design issue with your

HDTV or cell phone, the cost of a recall can be very expensive. As a result, companies seek to hire highly trained individuals to work on products with high impact or visibility, such as device programming in televisions, stereo systems, and telephones. This is not to say that individuals without a degree are never viable candidates for embedded systems development.

Core Requirements
- o BS or MS in electrical and electronic engineering or computer engineering
- o 3+ years' embedded design experience
- o 3+ years' C/C++ language experience

Elective Requirements
- o Windows CE development experience
- o ARM assembler programming experience
- o Real-time operating systems
- o Other experience based on the device (DSP, telephone, RFID)

Hiring Challenges

The challenge in software development is much the same as in IT in general, where fast-paced change is the name of the game. As fast as the changes come, developers must know how to keep the pace or else be quickly left behind. New development technologies are emerging every day, whether open-source or commercial. Developers everywhere have a long list of skills to stay current on.

With this challenge comes the difficulty for technical recruiters not only to keep pace with the changing technologies but to find developers who excel at all the current development technologies. The developer is either a jack-of-all-trades or a master of one, leaving the technical recruiters and hiring managers with a vital question to answer: whether to hire a person for their specific skills or overall performance. Unless there is a glut of unemployed skilled developers, this question must be answered by the hiring manager. When recruiters do not ask or have this question answered by hiring managers, it can lead to an unsuccessful search process.

Developers, in their search for a new company, are always on the lookout for organizations that utilize newer technologies and are also open to research. The newer the technologies used in a company, the more appealing the job becomes to the candidate. Imagine a candidate still working with Microsoft Windows NT 4.0 Server, SQL Server 7.0, or Exchange Server 5.0. Though the software is basically similar to their more recent versions, this candidate has very outdated skills. An organization utilizing more recent software versions would hesitate to hire this candidate.

The same is true for organizations that still use older versions of software. Candidates with newer skills would not touch them with a long pole except to come in and revamp and upgrade their systems. Some candidates stay away from companies with outdated systems, making them a hard sell for recruiters. Organizations seeking to attract the brightest candidates will want to be on the cutting edge of technology.

Staying Current

As people continuously seek more task efficiency and effectiveness, developers and the companies that hire them will always be searching for and creating new methodologies, technologies, and paradigms that make the process of development easier and faster. There will always be technologies out there that the average technical recruiter has never heard of or seen. For that reason, when you stumble upon a new term either in a job description or résumé of which you know nothing, the trick is to know where to find it and read about it.

One word—Google. One way to easily find the definition of a word without having to read a whole page is to go to Google and type "define [word in question]."

Furthermore, you can also subscribe to specific apps, news aggregation sites, or curated social media feeds. For example, Flipboard is an app that you can install or activate on your mobile device. When activated, choose topics including "technologies" that you would like to be current on. TechCrunch is a website that publishes current and trending technologies. One can either visit their website or follow their social media feeds. Flipboard and TechCrunch are just two examples of services that bring the information right to your fingertips.

What We Learned

- The two basic types of programming languages are low-level and high-level languages. Examples of low-level languages are machine language, assembly languages, and scripting languages.
- The low-level languages are so named because of their proximity to the processor. Similarly, high-level languages are so named because they are further away from the processor. Examples of high-level languages are Java and VB.NET.
- The types of software development are categorized by web development, applications development, systems development, and embedded systems development.
- Software development methodology is described as the processes used in creating software. The methodologies can either be plan driven or agile; examples include Agile, Rational Unified Process (RUP), Rapid Application Development (RAD), and Iterative. The one chosen by the development team depends on the team and the phase of the project in development.
- Development frameworks are like templates that developers use to jump-start their development. They include preestablished code that eliminates mundane tasks that would otherwise need

to be coded by the developer from the start. There are open-source frameworks as well as commercial grade ones. .NET framework and the PHP development framework are common examples.

- Staying current is a challenge for all parties: developers, hiring organizations, and recruiters. As the challenge deepens for developers and their organizations, recruiters must also seek ways to stay within the relevant technology corridor.

CHAPTER 8

SOFTWARE TESTING

In This Chapter

- software testing versus quality assurance
- the software tester's role
- types of testing
- skill sets for the tester
- software development engineer in test (SDET)
- a closer look at a software tester's job description
- reviewing candidates for software testing

Imagine how it would feel entering all your information into a form on a website, hitting the Submit button, and then seeing an error message requiring you to reenter all the information. Frustrating, to say the least, but this is how users feel each time they use inadequately tested software products. When web applications and electronic products are inappropriately tested, the company's integrity is at stake. This is one of the reasons proper testing is so important. It's the same reason companies dedicate time and resources to ensure the quality of their products.

In this chapter, we elaborate on software testing in the context of a job role. In addition, we compare software testing with quality assurance to identify the differences. After that, we examine some reasons testers prefer the title of "quality assurance analyst" rather than "software tester." Further sections in the chapter will review the role and skill sets of the software tester.

It is important for technical recruiters to understand software testing, its challenges, and its recruiting outlook for the coming years. If software development skills in .NET, Java, and SQL are still the most sought-after skills, then it makes sense that the testing of applications developed with these skill sets would be equally important.

What Is Software Testing?

Software testing is a process of verifying and validating that a software application works according to documented business specifications and technical requirements. Specifically, it is ensuring that the software is without defects, bugs, variances, or errors. Software bugs are inconsistencies or discrepancies causing software to behave in a way that was not documented in the specifications.

What Does a Software Tester Do?

According to Patton's (2006) book on software testing, the goal of a software tester is to find bugs, find them as early as possible, and make sure they get fixed. He lists the traits of software testers in terms of these categories:

- o Explorers: not afraid to venture into the unknown
- o Troubleshooters: good at figuring out why something does not work
- o Relentless: working tirelessly to find hidden bugs
- o Mellowed perfectionists: strive for perfection but know when to stop

    o   Tactful and diplomatic: knowing how to tactfully inform developers of the bad news when bugs are found

    o   Persuasive: good at demonstrating why a bug needs to be fixed

    o   Knowledgeable of software programming: knowledge in programming languages gives the tester further testing qualifications (i.e., an understanding of how software is written and, therefore, how to test it)

Software Testing versus Quality Assurance

Quality assurance is generally defined as a process of consistently setting and carrying out standards to monitor and improve the overall performance of a project, whereas software testing is seen as a segment of quality assurance that deals with checking a software program to ensure that it fulfills its intended purpose. In essence, quality assurance is a more holistic way of dealing with the overall objective of adhering to a set of defined quality standards, while software testing checks for defects in a product. The majority of the software testers I know (myself included, when I worked as one at Match.com) would like to see themselves as quality assurance analysts, even though 95 percent of the job they perform on a day-to-day basis is actually software testing.

No matter how many people are bent on differentiating software testing and quality assurance, the technical recruiter should stay away from this muddle unless it involves higher salaries for your candidates. If a candidate prefers the title "quality assurance analyst," then refer to the person as such. The same holds true for the "software tester" title.

There are times when employers use one title or the other. This depends on a number of reasons, ranging from visibility of the job on the job board to how much they are willing to pay for the more respectable-sounding title. There was an instance at a company I once worked at where the title "report writer" was changed to "SQL Server data analyst" to attract more candidates—and it worked. The content of the job description was the same. The only change was the title, but as a result, the résumés started coming in.

Consider the titles software tester and quality assurance analyst. Which one do you think a candidate would prefer to have on his or her business card? I think the title "quality assurance analyst" wins the day and attracts more remuneration.

The Software Tester's Role

Although the difference between a software tester and a quality assurance analyst is sometimes only in the title, in other cases, there are actual differences in the tasks. Software testing is the process of testing software to ensure that it is working according to specifications. The tester validates and verifies that a software application or process meets the specific objectives of its intended purpose. The software tester must be very knowledgeable about the business and technical requirements of a product in order to test software appropriately. Some of the software tester's required skills may depend on the specifics of the software environment. However, the basic skill set is the same and includes, for example, writing test plans, finding important defects, and patience when working with developers.

The software tester is an inquisitive person who is able to find the one bad apple in the midst of thousands of good ones. The software tester should also be detail oriented. He or she knows that questioning everything is the one sure way to make sure no problem slips by unnoticed.

The software tester works for a lot of people in the development team, including the following:

o Business analysts (BAs), who write product specifications and their use cases. The software tester liaises with BAs to ensure that they understand the product functionalities and can therefore devise appropriate test plans. The BA sometimes acts as a go-between for the tester and programmer when discrepancies occur in how functionalities are perceived to work.

o Project managers (PMs) want to know as soon as possible if the project is being delayed as a result of a defect. The tester works with PMs to ensure they understand the time frame of the project and then works within this time frame in creating test plans, executing tests, and reporting on defects.

o Developers or programmers also want to know as soon as a defect or bug is discovered in a system. Depending on the test-reporting process in a company, the tester passes or fails a test and directs the failed test to the developer to fix the problem. The process is repeated as needed until the project has passed most tests and is deemed both bug-free and working according to specifications.

Software Testing Team Members

Even though the software tester interfaces with other members of the software development team, the software testing core team consists of other software testers, a test manager, and a code configuration manager. In recent years, a DevOps professional is also part of this team. In some organizations, the DevOps person has taken over the role of the code configuration manager. Working with a team, the DevOps professional's job is to ensure that the software testing process is performed well. Figure 8.1 shows the members of the software testing team.

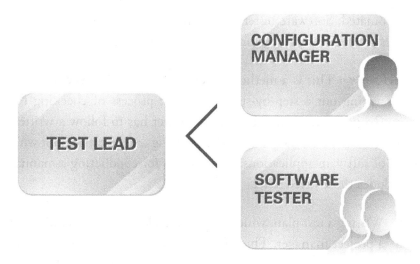

Figure 8.1. Other software testing team members

Test manager: This person handles resource planning, resource utilization, and work forecasts. The lead works with the database administrators and systems administrators in setting up the test environment and the performing data refresh. The lead is often the person who presents the status reports to the project managers and other stakeholders. They communicate and escalate any testing concerns from team members to appropriate leads.

DevOps / code configuration manager: This person merges and integrates (continuous integration) code changes in all environments (development, testing, and production). He or she performs continuous builds (a.k.a. continuous delivery) and release management within the production environment. The DevOps/CCM person uses several automation tools to perform source code management, builds, releases, and deployment of software, such as Jenkins, Puppet, and Chef.

Types of Testing

In this section, we review software testing types, which are different from the testing methods. There are two methods of testing: manual and automated. Software testers either manually test with their hands and eyes or write code to perform tests more quickly.

Manual testing: This is a method of testing that involves the software tester carrying out a step-by-step systematic process of checking for defects. To perform manual testing, the tester has to follow a written plan referred to as the *test plan*. Manual testing can be carried out with the aid of software applications. The process for conducting a manual test includes those listed here:

o   Writing a test plan, which is the equivalent of a project plan for a project manager. This includes the purpose and scope of the test; features to be tested; the strategy, resources, and testing methods to be deployed; the test tools; pass and fail criteria; the deliverables; and the start and end dates.
o   Writing detailed test cases that illustrate step-by-step actions to be taken by the tester and also the expected results.
o   Executing the steps in the test cases.
o   Documenting the test report.

Automated testing: This is a method of testing in which a software tool actually does the testing instead of a person. There are cases when this method of testing is better than manual testing. Some reasons for utilizing automated tests are as follows:

o   The ability to run many functional tests at any time of day and quickly;
o   To ensure thoroughness and accuracy when tests are run repeatedly over time; and
o   To free up software testers from repetitive testing so they can concentrate on more creative or strategic quality initiatives.

Types of software testing are classified according to the purpose of the test. The purpose of the test forms the basis of the type of test. For example, if the purpose is to test the performance of a given application, the type of test is called a *performance test*. Other software testing types are described below and include black-box testing, white-box testing, gray-box testing, functional testing, regression testing, smoke testing, and stress testing.

Black-box testing: This type of testing approach is called black box because the tester does not have access to the inner workings of the software and tests only how the software functions. For example, in testing a member registration web form, the black-box tester enters first and last names, addresses, and contact information values into a web form in different orders and expects certain results. Figure 8.2 displays a simple example of a web form test using black-box testing.

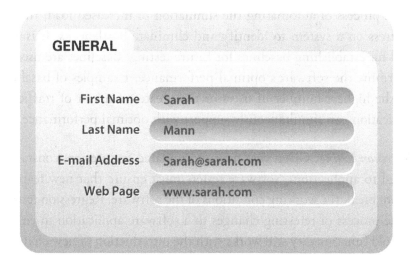

Figure 8.2. Black-box testing of a web form

White-box testing: This requires some programming or software development skills. In this type of testing approach, the tester has some knowledge about the inner workings of the code and can manipulate the code to generate different results. This type of testing is usually performed by software testers with programming experience.

Gray-box testing: This is a hybrid of black-box and white-box testing. A testing approach is referred to as *gray box* when both black- and white-box testing approaches are used.

Functional testing: Functional testing can sometimes be referred to as *black-box testing*. This software testing focuses on the functions of a program to ensure it works according to the specifications. Functional tests are carried out with the end user in mind. This type of test confirms that the application performs according to user expectations.

Performance testing: There are times when web-based applications accept hundreds of thousands of hits simultaneously. During the testing of the application, it may be impossible to manually simulate the amount of expected load/traffic on the software in order to experience possible bottlenecks that exist in the software. Performance testing is the process of automating the simulation of increased load, traffic, or stress on a system to identify and eliminate bottlenecks. It is also used for establishing baselines for future testing. Baselines are used to determine the software's optimal performance. Examples of baselines are the highest number of users or the greatest amount of traffic an application can simultaneously support with optimal performance.

Regression testing: Given that new and updated features are constantly added to applications, software testers must ensure that new features do not break the working conditions of the software. Regression testing is the process of retesting changes to a software application to ensure that old functionality still works with the introduction of new changes.

Smoke testing: This is quick testing performed on a piece of software to verify that major functionalities of the software work well. Verifying the major components of a simple web-based application could include verifying (1) that new users are still able to register and (2) that buttons actually perform their intended functions. This type of test is by no means exhaustive. The term *smoke testing* was first derived from the hardware industry, which suggests that hardware equipment has passed its initial test if there is no smoke after it is powered up.

Stress testing: This is the process of testing a system to evaluate factors that might break the system—the conditions under which a system fails and how it fails. There are many creative ways to fail a system, including running processes that deplete the resources available for other computer operations or purposely stopping a required service. The objective of the stress test is to find out how a system responds to failure. Removal of the failure-causing element resulting in a more robust system is the desired result of this type of testing.

Stages of Software Testing

Software testing has stages that define the various activities that are performed to start and complete a software testing cycle. These activities fall into the test planning, test analysis, test design, and verification categories.

Test planning: Software testing may seem like a simple and straightforward task, but in reality, it is not. There are many moving parts that require the availability of a test plan. This test plan can include various parts such as the ones below.

- Type of tests: functionality, performance, or a combination
- Scope of software: testing of individual features or all features
- Resources availability
- Test schedule and budget

Though the software testing manager and the project manager are responsible for formulating this plan, any experienced software tester can produce the plan with help from the project manager. The project manager is involved in ensuring that the budget and schedule are aligned with the overall project plan. This plan is usually written in accordance with the product specifications as well as business requirement sign-offs and approvals.

Test analysis: This stage occurs before the beginning of the coding stage in the software development life cycle (SDLC) process. This is when decisions are made regarding the mechanism (manual or automated) and types of testing required for each stage of the SDLC. Test cases are created at this stage. The test cases describe the items to be tested and the steps to be followed to verify the software according to business requirements and specifications. The test cases are usually written by the software testers who will be performing the actual tests.

Test design: "This stage is mostly a revision-and-review stage" where documents from the planning and analysis stages are revised, reviewed, and signed off on by the business analysts, project managers, and testing managers. This stage also includes preparing all test data and scripts in readiness for test execution.

Verification: Test execution starts at this stage. Functionality, performance, stress, and regression tests are performed using automated and (or) manual tests. Defects and bugs are identified and reported, and the testing process continues.

Testing Skill Sets

Software testing can be exhilarating, especially when an important defect is found. Here are some very basic skill sets a software tester must possess:

o   Must be able to describe the testing process. Whatever the level of the tester, the ability to understand and describe a testing process is expected.
o   Must understand the software development life cycle (SDLC) and where testing falls within the process.
o   Should be able to describe the difference between black-box, white-box, and gray-box testing.
o   Experience with at least one software testing tool.
o   Should have a good technical background. A person cannot really test software if they do not have the appropriate technical background.

   o   Experience with at least two or three types of testing, including automated, regression, functionality, and performance testing.

   o   Some level of experience writing test plans and test cases.

Software Tester Profile
- Six years of experience in software testing, software engineering, and SDLC on multiple platforms in various industries.
- Extensive experience executing both manual and automated testing on e-business/e-commerce, desktop, and client-server applications.
- Experience in testing Java Enterprise Edition (JEE), VB.NET, C#, and ASP.NET-based applications on Linux/UNIX (for JEE) and Windows platforms.
- Extensive experience in performing data validation and manipulation using T-SQL on SQL Server and PL/SQL on Oracle.
- Experience developing test plans and test cases for functional, security, integration, regression, load, performance, and usability (UAT) testing.
- Experience creating test automation harnesses for regression testing

Technical Skills
- Test Tools: WinRunner, QTP, LoadRunner, Test Director, Quality Center.
- Databases: Oracle 11i, PL/SQL, SQL Server, T-SQL, SSRS, MS Access.
- Operating Systems: Windows Server, UNIX/Linux.
- Technologies: .NET (C#, VB.NET), JEE, Web services, Remoting, C++, VB Script, JavaScript.
- Methodologies: Waterfall, Extreme Programming, Agile.

Professional Experience
- Ensured that overall manual and automated testing ratio was maintained at 50:50.
- Created test cases based on application functionalities.

- Responsible for preparing and presenting weekly progress reports on testing activities within the team.
- Performed black-box/regression and white-box testing on online subscription applications that included web services, APIs and remoting, and message queuing.
- Worked with developers to resolve identified defects.
- Verified data integrity using T-SQL queries and validated test results with the expected results.
- Used Quick Test Professional (QTP) for regression testing of new builds.
- Developed UAT test scripts for new functionalities

Figure 8.3. Sample software tester résumé

Looking at figure 8.3, you can see that the software skill sets found on a software tester's résumé can sometimes be similar to those of a programmer. The differences lie in their level of experience and how the knowledge is utilized. Most testers are like consultants, who have experience and knowledge in a wide range of environments and technologies but do not have the depth to actually write code or do development. The trend is shifting just a bit; these days, you may find a number of software testers who were formerly software developers. Their reasons for transitioning to testing may range from burnout to simple preference. The developer-turned-tester may excel in white- and gray-box testing, where the individual can leverage his or her development skills.

A Closer Look at a Software Tester's Job Description

When you study any job description, there are always key skills that you pay close attention to. As you identify them, mark or underline these skills, as they will form the must-haves for the job role. Following the guidelines in the "Anatomy of a Technical Job Requisition" section found in chapter 1 of this book, you may want to find out more about this job description from the hiring manager.

Depending on your experience in recruiting for a particular job role, reviewing a job description for a position you have recruited for several times before may become an automatic process for you. This is because you now know all the requirements by heart, especially if the position is for an established client or a chosen industry vertical, such as legal, medical, hospitality, or government.

Looking at the software tester job description in figure 8.4, you will notice that the must-haves have been identified with underlining; these are the points that will be further analyzed. When analyzing a job description, the two questions you ask yourself are "Why does the hiring manager want this skill?" and "How will this skill help the candidate perform better at this job?"

SAMPLE

> **Software Tester Job Description**
> The software tester will test and verify software products before they launch.
> **Responsibilities**
> (1) <u>Work closely with development</u>, project management, marketing, and other groups.
> (2) Provide scopes, <u>test plan</u>, and <u>test cases</u> to the QA manager and all QA team members involved in the project.
> (3) <u>Present the test plans</u> and test cases to the QA team.
> (4) Ensure usability and customer experience is covered in all test cases and test plans.
> (5) Participate in all <u>code reviews</u> pertaining to the project.
> (6) <u>Justify the business impact</u> for each change or bug found.
> (7) Regression/stress test the applications with any regression testing tools.
> **Requirements**
> (1) 3+ years' software testing experience
> (2) 2+ years' experience in <u>T-SQL programming</u>
> (3) 2+ years' experience in testing C#, VB.NET applications
> (4) 2+ years' experience in automated testing

Figure 8.4. Sample job description for a software tester

Responsibilities and Requirements Analysis

Let's begin by analyzing the responsibilities and requirements identified in the sample job description for a software tester in figure 8.4. After the analysis, you will be able to communicate better with the candidate and identify at the outset whether a candidate meets the needs of the position. The candidate, in turn, will respect your grasp of your client's technology environment and will likely open up more to you because he or she will feel that the two of you are on similar wavelengths.

Work with developers. Because the tester's job is to find errors (whether bugs or defects) made by developers, the inherent relationship between these two groups is usually just a little contentious. Though each group makes a great effort to mask this contention, it's still a little difficult for some developers when informed (maybe more than once) that their code was "bug-ful." With this in mind, there must be a peer relationship between the testers and developers whereby the testers are not afraid to voice their opinions and communicate on product requirements and user expectations. Testers must be confident in their abilities and not see themselves as mere bug finders but as key members of the development team whose full participation is required and expected.

Test plans / test cases. Testers must be able to write test plans and test cases to support the product specifications. Companies usually have templates from which all test plans and cases must be written. The test case documentation must be very comprehensive to cover every use case scenario of the product being tested. Testers must also be able to present these documents to their team for peer review.

Code reviews. The audience for code reviews used to be only developers, but now that the software testing process starts from the very beginning of the product cycle, testers are encouraged and required to participate in the review of developers' code. In this review, developers reveal the flow and reasoning behind their code for the review of their peers. Software testers are not required or expected to critique the code but rather to listen and understand the inner workings of the software development for white-box testing.

Justify business impact of defects. Pointing out another person's mistakes is very easy and comes easily to most human beings. One lesson that software testers have learned only too well is to be able to find the important defects at the onset of testing. The important bugs might be subjective and based on the tester (and may not be as important to one tester as to another), so in order to eliminate such subjectivity, the tester must be able to write a justification of why a given defect must be fixed and the impact it will have on the overall product if left unfixed.

T-SQL programming experience. This experience is required for white-box testing of the database systems used for software applications.

Reviewing a Software Tester

Once a technical recruiter understands software testing as a whole, it becomes easier to go through the qualification process of ensuring that a particular candidate is better suited to a certain job. Software testing is one of those straightforward positions to recruit for.

The skill sets are mostly tools based; this means that when the software tester is very knowledgeable in a software testing tool, the other skill sets will be easier to acquire if they are not already there. With a great percentage of software becoming web based, there is a bigger demand for software testers with web testing experience than with traditional non-web-based software.

For instance, a software tester with six years' experience in the telecommunications hardware industry may not be the right candidate for a web applications company. The mismatch can be identified in several ways, such as during the review of the candidate's résumé or in conversation to find out about his or her experience in a specific mode and pace of testing. Table 8.1 displays key differences between a tester with telecom experience versus one with web applications experience.

Differentiators	Telecommunications Company	Web Applications Company
Testing cycles	Once every month or two months	Twice a week
Test without test plans	Must have a traditional documented test plan and test cases that have been signed off on by stakeholders before testing commences	Tester in this environment must be able to perform tests without a test plan.
Release cycles	Once a month/quarter	Once or twice a week
Pace	Slow and steady	Very fast paced, though sometimes there's not much to do
Average hours	40 hours per week	45 to 50 hours per week
Software	Operating system-based software tools, more specialized tools	.NET, Java, Windows, UNIX/Linux, readily available web application tools

Table 8.1. Differentiators between software testers with telecom experience versus web applications experience

When a software tester's résumé reports that there were software releases or testing cycles once or twice per week, that's a very clear indication that the candidate worked for a fast-paced company. This indication will help the recruiter identify the environment that best suits the candidate and the hiring company alike.

Questions for the Candidate

There are many software-testing interview questions one can ask a candidate. Here are a few simple questions that will give the recruiter a feel for the technical and overall fit of the software tester.

- "Explain your typical software-testing environment."
  - o The answers here should touch on how many testers, how many other software programmers, SDLC, white-box/black-box testing, and automated/manual testing.
- "In a typical month, how many release/testing cycles did your last company have on a weekly basis?"
  - o The answers will tell you the pace of the development cycle.
  - o If the answer to the above question is from one to two cycles per week, then there is a high possibility that the tester did not have the time to write test plans or test cases for each of the tests. The follow-up question would then be ... you guessed it:
- "How often did you write test plans/test cases for the tests you ran?"
- "Of all the testing you performed at this company, what was the ratio of automated versus manual testing, or what percentage was manual and what percentage was automated?"
  - o Because testers are not programmers, some testers fail to acknowledge any automated projects performed in the past for fear of being branded an automated tester. Automation skill is a great skill to have as a tester, so as a recruiter, you want to ensure that you capture this experience (no matter how limited).
- "How much experience do you have with back-end testing, especially with T-SQL?"
  - o Figure 8.5 is a set of T-SQL sample questions to ask your candidates to ensure that they have basic experience with T-SQL. Here are the answers:
    - ▪ question 1: five columns and six rows
    - ▪ question 2: EID (The reason is that this column qualifies as a unique column and therefore is the column that identifies the row.)
    - ▪ question 3: SELECT * FROM Employee, or SELECT EID, First, Last, City, Position FROM Employee
    - ▪ question 4: UPDATE Employee SET City = 'New York'

Review the table and answer the following questions.

Table name: Employee

EID	First	Last	City	Position
1001	Kelli	Clark	New York	Manager
1002	Sophie	Herring	New York	Accountant
1003	John	Henry	Dallas	Manager
1004	Vin	Redding	Austin	Customer service rep
1005	James	Wesley	Cleveland	System admin
1007	Jose	Cruz	New York	Manager

(1) How many columns and rows does this table have?
(2) In the table above (named Employee), which column would be the primary key and why?
(3) Write a query to get all of the table's records.
(4) Write a query to update the table so that all employees live in the same city—New York.

Figure 8.5. Sample prescreen questions for software testers involved in data validation

Software Development Engineer in Test (SDET)

Early in the chapter, we touched on the existence of software testers who also have experience in software development. The title of this type of software tester is software development engineer in test (SDET). In terms of prioritization of job functions, the SDET is first and foremost a software tester with emphasis on software quality, and then a software developer. This means that the SDET's role as a tester supersedes that of a developer. Hence, the SDET's skill sets are primarily those of a tester who also possesses good programming skill sets. These programming skill sets are used to write scripts that automate tests. The following are typical responsibilities and requirements of an SDET.

Responsibilities

- o Responsible for improving application quality by building automated solutions and frameworks to test software products
- o Responsible for creating automated testing solutions from technical designs and specifications
- o Responsible for writing test cases for automated tests
- o Executes automated tests using Selenium, Cucumber, and Java
- o Performs reviews of automation and application code

Requirements

- o 3+ years of experience in automation testing
- o 3+ years of experience in software development or software testing development
- o Exposure to continuous integration/continuous delivery (DevOps: Jenkins)
- o Experience with Java, J2EE, Spring, or other MVC framework and ORM Frameworks
- o Experience with databases such as MS SQL, Oracle/MySQL, NoSQL

Reviewing the responsibilities of and requirements for an SDET, you notice the emphasis on delivering quality software through test automation. Since SDETs are also software developers, they use that experience to write automated testing scripts that rapidly verify the quality, robustness, and performance of the software product.

What We Learned

- • Software testing is a process of verifying and validating that a software application works in accordance with documented business specifications and technical requirements and is without defects, bugs, variances, or errors.

- Software bugs are inconsistencies or discrepancies in software causing it to act in a way that was not included or documented in the specifications or simply to not work properly.
- The goal of the software tester is to find bugs, find them as early as possible, and make sure they get fixed. The software tester's role is to validate and verify that a software application or process meets the specific objectives of its intended purpose. The individual filling this role must be very knowledgeable about the business and technical requirements of a product in order to test it appropriately. Some of the tools/skills the tester must have may depend on the specific software environment, but the basic skill sets are the same: writing test plans, finding important defects, and patience when working with developers.
- Types of software testing are classified according to the purpose of the test. Software testing types include black-box testing, white-box testing, gray-box testing, stress testing, regression testing, and functional testing.
- The two methods of testing are manual and automated testing. Software testers either manually test with their hands and eyes or write code to perform tests automatically.
- Software testing has stages that define the various activities that are performed to start and complete a software testing cycle. These activities fall into the test planning, test analysis, test design, and verification categories.
- A software development engineer in test (SDET) possesses a combination of software testing and software development skill sets. The primary responsibility of an SDET is to improve software quality by building automated solutions and frameworks to test software products.

CHAPTER 9

TRADITIONAL DATABASE TECHNOLOGIES

In This Chapter

- traditional database applications
- database objects
- database technologies
- database job roles

It's said that information is power. Well, building a database is the first step in obtaining this power. Most if not all web applications have a database behind the scenes. They collect data such as first name, last name, email address, zip code, and so on. How data is stored, for how long, and how data is retrieved and manipulated to provide decision-making information are questions we answer in this chapter.

This chapter also discusses traditional databases and the many aspects of database technologies used in business intelligence, reporting, database development, administration, data warehousing, and data mining.

Nontraditional database technologies and big data technologies and are discussed in chapter 10.

Traditional Database Applications

Traditional database applications fall into two main categories, and their characteristics have a strong effect on how they are designed and implemented. The two are online transaction processing (OLTP) and online analytical processing (OLAP), which can also be referred to as a decision support system.

Online transaction processing: OLTP database applications are great for managing changing data. A typical OLTP application has many users who perform simultaneous transactions in which data is changed in real time. Common examples of these types of databases are airline ticketing systems and banking transaction systems.

Online analytical processing: Decision-support database applications are best for running queries that do not change data. Common examples of these types of database applications are found in business intelligence applications that allow a company's senior management to run reports (querying the data) that summarize its sales data by date, region, product, store, and salesperson. This enables management to determine trends in sales quickly and make business decisions.

Database Objects

Database objects are the tangible components that make up a database. The database developer (a.k.a. database engineer, DBE) creates database objects. The database administrator (DBA) maintains and supports them. Some of the objects that make up the database are tables, stored procedures, views, and triggers.

Database objects are created using a language called Structured Query Language or SQL (pronounced "sequel"). It is a standard language for accessing and manipulating database systems. The American National Standards Institute (ANSI) adopted SQL as a standard in 1986.

Tables: These are database objects that contain rows and columns. These rows and columns store the attributes of an item. For example, if *Customer* is a table name, the table stores all the attributes of customers, such as company name, contact name, address, phone number, and email address.

Stored procedures: Sometimes called *procs*, these are the most-used programmatic objects in a database. They are a collection of SQL statements saved and executed automatically in the database.

Views: These are queries that act like a window to an underlying table. They have rows and columns just like a table. Views act as a middleman between the user and the table, ensuring a sort of security buffer by hiding the structure of the table from end users. The purpose is to prevent end users from changing the structure of the table or deleting the table.

Triggers: Triggers are special types of stored procedures that automatically execute in response to an event that occurs in the database.

Database Technologies

Let's explore how database technologies are applied. As many as four or five of the terms in this section can be found in any database-related job description. Therefore, it's important for a technical recruiter to become familiar with the terms and how they are used in the database work environment.

Business Intelligence

Business intelligence (BI) is knowledge derived from in-depth analysis of an organization's business data; it is usually stored in a data warehouse. In some cases, business intelligence is a classier name for a robust reporting system. A database is only as good as the information that can be derived from it in the form of reporting and business intelligence.

For example, you make decisions at the end of the year or the beginning of the next year when your credit card company sends you a summary of your spending habits. From looking at it, you see that you spent too much money at a particular retailer or that your entertainment choices were too expensive. Now, you can make a *decision* based on the information. For example, you can decide to limit your entertainment in the coming year or cut down on your clothing purchases. These are very simple implementations of how a good reporting system can help you make decisions. Now imagine how important business intelligence can be to a major retailer or gas-dispensing company.

The typical job titles in the realms of BI and reporting are business intelligence analyst, business intelligence specialist, and SQL reporting analyst. A BI or database reporting analyst must know the business and understand the flow of data (where it comes from, how it is manipulated, and where it ends up) in order to create decision support or BI systems. This person should have a good understanding of the database languages—T-SQL, PL/SQL, and MySQL—and also the reporting or BI applications used by the company.

Some BI positions require candidates with a statistics background. People with this background tend to be able to find more trends in data. This is not to say that people without this background do not make great analysts.

Database Reporting

Although the impact of reporting in an organization has been explained in the context of BI, it's still worth noting that reporting has its own separate knowledge base and skill sets. An organization may have a good reporting system without having implemented the enhanced tools that create the BI aspect.

In a case like this, reporting is the ability to analyze data in order to answer simple questions such as "Of the people that registered on the website, how many live in Dallas and are male?" At the very least, every database system should have good reporting and search functionalities. Retrieving information from a database system requires a good understanding of the data structure. This is why reporting candidates require time (sometimes as much as two weeks) to understand the data structure, objects, and business rules before they can start reporting.

A good reporting system is very important to any organization. Business determinations and decisions are made based on information gathered from database systems. Some organizational decisions are backed by information gathered from database reporting systems with the help of a reporting analyst or BI analysts. Though we talk about the reporting analyst skill set later, a recruiter might consider saying to a reporting analyst, "Describe a time when a change was made by the organization's decision makers as a result of your business and data reporting."

"Describe a time when a change was made by the organization's decision makers as a result of your business and data reporting."

CALL NOTES

Data Mining

This is the process of knowledge discovery or retrieval of hidden information from data. Data can be mined whether it is stored in spreadsheets, tables, or plain text. It is the process of sifting through large amounts of data to produce relationships, patterns, or trends that might be of value to the organization for producing models and forecasting.

Retailers such as Starbucks and Wal-Mart, which use data mining may notice the buying patterns of their customers and then make decisions to better their product placements. For example, a business problem might be: how can a retailer sell more of one product to its customers? This could be translated into a data mining problem such as: which customers are most likely to purchase the product? A model that predicts the customers that are most likely to purchase the product is built using data comprising of customers' past purchases.

Extract, Transform, and Load (ETL)

ETL is a process of loading data into a data warehouse or other data repository. It involves three steps. First, extract data from different and disparate sources. Second, transform the data to fit business needs or storage requirements. Third, load the data into a database or data warehouse. Figure 9.1 illustrates the steps in the ETL process and how it starts with extracting and ends with loading.

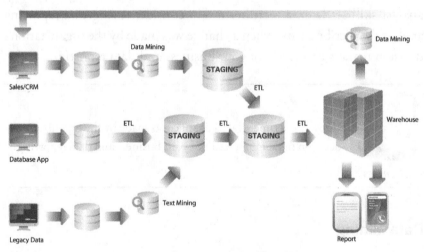

Figure 9.1. Extraction, transformation, and loading

Database Normalization

Normalization is a logical database design process that involves using formal methods to separate data into multiple related tables to reduce redundant data, thereby adding flexibility and consistency to the table. Reasonable normalization frequently improves performance. This is because only related data is stored in a table, which makes it easier and quicker to retrieve data, resulting in improved performance.

Data Warehouse

A data warehouse (DW) is a read-only repository for an organization's historical data. Data mining functions are usually performed on the data warehouse by data analysts to find business trends. An organization might use the data warehouse to discover what day of the week a particular product was most sold in the previous quarter. It provides a multidimensional view of an organization's data.

Data Modeling

Data modeling is the process of designing the structure and flow of data within a given system and includes logical data modeling, physical data modeling, and architectural data modeling. Data modeling is used for creating a high-level description and overview of the properties that make up the flow of data in an information system. Examples of data modeling software include Embarcadero ER/Studio and ERWin.

UML (Unified Modeling Language)

UML is the industry standard language for specifying, visualizing, and documenting components of a software system. UML is used for business process modeling, systems engineering modeling, and for creating organizational structures. It can also be used for data modeling.

MySQL

MySQL (pronounced "my sequel") is an open-source relational database management system that has become very popular for creating web-based database applications. It is the database component of the LAMP (Linux, Apache, MySQL, and PHP) web development solutions.

Database Job Roles

Database roles are defined differently in each organization. A database administrator in one organization may include three separate roles—database development, database reporting, and database administration—whereas it may involve only one role in another organization.

Next, we will examine the job roles of the reporting analyst, database developer, database administrator, business intelligence specialist, and data warehouse consultant. We will evaluate their specific responsibilities, requirements, and questions you might ask candidates.

Database Administration

Database administration (DBA) is the support, maintenance, and management of a database system. The tasks involved are usually process driven, ranging from system configuration and break-fix to acquiring new hardware. A few years back, some companies combined the tasks of database administration and database development and sought to find candidates who could perform both. You may still find the occasional SQL developer/DBA job titles, but most companies recognize the difference and separate the job roles. Administration involves configuration, maintenance, and troubleshooting, while development involves programming skills.

Database Development

The process of designing *containers* that collect different attributes of a system is the job of a database developer. A database developer with a good understanding of the business requirements defines the kinds of data attributes that must be collected and the relationships among the attributes. The database developer writes code for collecting the data as well as the code that fulfills business rules and requirements.

A Closer Look at Database Roles

A job description provides information to the recruiter about the skill sets sought after by an organization. It also provides information pertaining to the organization's technical environment. It is easier to identify the needs and wants of a hiring manager by underlining or highlighting specific skill sets in the job description. In this section, we examine database roles and then look at sample recruiter questions.

Database Engineer (DBE)

The DBE designs database solutions that solve data problems. To this end, the DBE designs, develops, and maintains database solutions for an OLTP database. The DBE's tasks revolve around creating stored procedures and functions that interact with the underlying tables and the application tier.

In figure 9.2, a typical job description for a SQL Server developer, some duties and responsibilities have been underlined. The underlined terms will be explained in the section below.

Database Developer

Provide expert database design, development, and implementation using Microsoft SQL Server.
 	
Duties and Responsibilities:
  (1) Develop and document <u>data migration</u> strategies and <u>ETL</u> plans.
  (2) Develop complex SQL scripts to support other development teams.
  (3) <u>Optimize and tune</u> SQL statements and databases.
  (4) Perform database <u>infrastructure design</u> and <u>automation of data loads.</u>
  (5) Troubleshoot and resolve database issues.
  (6) Manage the database development, quality assurance, and production database environments and manage application upgrades on them.
  (7) Support internal clients by creating data-driven applications/ reports and ad hoc queries.
 	
Qualifications and Requirements:
  (1) BS in computer science, mathematics, or engineering.
  (2) 4+ years' experience working as a database developer with SQL Server.
  (3) Experience with SQL Server <u>SSIS</u>
  (4) Must have demonstrated understanding of <u>logical</u> and <u>physical database design</u> for <u>transactional</u>, <u>data warehouse</u>, and data (de) <u>normalization</u> concepts
  (5) Deep knowledge and proven experience working in advanced T-SQL
  (6) Experience with SQL Server Reporting Services
  (7) Experience in business <u>requirement analysis</u> and conversion to database design
  (8) Experience with <u>business intelligence</u> products such as Business Objects

Figure 9.2. Typical job description for a SQL Server developer

Responsibilities Analysis

Having been on both sides of the recruiting spectrum—as a candidate as well as a technical recruiter—I know how important it is for a technical recruiter to understand the reasons driving specific skill requirements. The recruiter who understands these drivers wins the respect of both the candidates and hiring managers. The recruiter is able to communicate better with the candidates and can identify at the outset whether a candidate meets the requirements. The candidate, in turn, will respect the recruiter's grasp of the client's technology environment and therefore be more open to the recruiter.

With this in mind, let's analyze the skill sets found in a database engineer's job description and why organizations require these skills.

Data migration is the process of copying or moving data from one database system to another. The movement of data may be from disparate systems, such as from Oracle to SQL Server. It may also be from similar systems, such as from one SQL Server database to another SQL Server database. The process of migration is not complete until the data has been tested or validated to ensure its integrity and reliability; therefore, the database developer has to develop scripts (e.g., checksum scripts) to validate its reliability.

> *Why is this skill required?* Part of a database developer's task deals with knowing the data provenance (origins), where it ends up, and how to manipulate the data to fit the organization's requirements. Sometimes the data may be stored in another format. The database developer must know how to move (or migrate) this data from one point to the other. There's always more than one way to perform a task, so the developer must be able to document a best-practice strategy for performing this task in the organization.

ETL is the process of extracting, transforming, and loading data from disparate sources to its destination source. A migration process (previously described) can also include ETL processes.

Why is this skill required? The developer should have experience extracting and transforming data from different sources and then loading it into the destination database table(s).

Tuning and optimizing: Just as a car has to go through periodic tuning by a mechanic that understands its internal workings, so it is with a database system. After a period of continuous smooth running, the database objects need some tuning. Sometimes the tuning may be required as a result of poor initial design, in which case the developer corrects it.

Why is this skill required? Databases like Oracle Database or Microsoft SQL Server come with tools that allow technologists to optimize or tune the database. The developer needs to know how to use these tools to tune database objects.

Infrastructure design is the process of defining and creating the source, destination, interoperability, and connectivity of all the moving parts of a particular database solution. The developer diagrammatically defines the source, destination, and mutual relationship of all the tables as well as the views, stored procedures, triggers, and replication involved in a given solution.

Why is this skill required? It's crucial that the developer know how to design a solution from beginning to end—even more so for a developer who is familiar with the data environment than for a developer who just started at a company.

Automation of data loads involves the use of SSIS—SQL Server Integration Services—to load data into database tables. These tools can be used to automate the processes of locating the data source, extracting the raw data, transforming (scrubbing) it to an acceptable format, and then loading it into the database.

Why is this skill required? All the processes involved in migrating, transforming, and loading data can be automated with tools. Being able to use these tools to perform these tasks saves time and reduces the load on the database server. This skill is seen as a core requirement for any database developer.

Qualifications Analysis

SSIS: SQL Server Integration Services is an enhanced ETL tool in later versions of SQL Server. This is a core skill requirement.

Logical database design: The logical design of the database involves the implementation of tables and the relationships between them. This is a core requirement for creating relational databases. A good logical database design can lay the foundation for optimal database and application performance. A poor logical database design can hinder the performance of the whole system.

Physical database design: This describes how a database system will be physically implemented in order to meet its logical requirements. The performance of any database depends on the effective configuration of the physical design structures, including indexes, clustered indexes, indexed views, and partitions. The purpose of these physical structures is to enhance the performance and manageability of databases.

Normalizing and denormalizing: These are performed during the logical database design. They involve using methods to separate data into multiple related tables. When a database is designed properly, normalization improves its performance.

Requirements analysis: This is the determination of the needs and conditions to be met for a new or updated system. This analysis is usually documented in a use case and (or) product specifications document. The database developer often designs a database based on this document.

Résumé Phrases, Database Engineer

Designed and implemented a highly normalized membership registration database that contained approximately one thousand stored procedures and three hundred tables. Created custom replication scripts of production databases to the reporting and read servers.

Keywords of note: design database solution, custom replication, stored procedure.

Figure 9.3. Phrases on a database engineer's résumé

Recruiter Conversation with a Database Engineer

The following are some questions a technical recruiter might ask database engineers in order to understand their focus. Some candidates feel that recruiters do not have adequate knowledge of the intricacies of their technical skills. That's why we start this recruiter-to-candidate conversation with a tone that makes the candidate feel like they can actually relate to the recruiter.

The recruiter may start by going through the preliminaries of basic recruiter and candidate greetings and then flow right into the interview.

QUESTIONS

Greeting:
"Hi. My name is Helen Olive from ABC Solutions. I saw your résumé online and wanted to find out more about your skill sets in relation to a position I have today …. Is this okay?"

Interview:

"I enjoy listening to how programmers solve business problems with code. I'm going to ask you some general questions; your answers will give me a better understanding of what you do and perhaps what you enjoy the most in your job. Is that okay with you?"

(1) "Please describe your database environment ... your development, testing, and perhaps production environments."

(2) "Within SQL Server databases, there are tools and tasks that include SSIS, SSRS, notification services, replication, performance tuning, and database design solutions. Which of these do you enjoy the most?"

(3) "Which of the SQL Server tools do you use on a day-to-day basis and for what types of solutions?"

(4) "Describe a database application or feature you developed or assisted in developing. What problems did that application or feature solve? What were the considerations around this feature or design?"

(5) "What is the frequency of code propagation to your production environment?"

The above questions are all Microsoft SQL Server–centric. These tools and experiences can be replaced to suit other database technologies where applicable. The questions here are designed to reveal the experience level of the developer and match their experiences with the requirements of the hiring manager. The following are some reasons that motivate the questions.

Reason for question (1): This tells the recruiter about the database environment, the size of the team (e.g., whether this was a two-person or twenty-person database development team), and whether processes were followed for development (such as SDLC or any other process). It will also give the recruiter a window on whether the candidate understands the inner workings of the development team. The answers here should include how many servers were available in the testing and production environments as well as the platform supported and whether it was Windows, UNIX, both, or another combination.

Reason for question (2): Except for SSRS, the answers here should include all the tools and tasks outlined in this question. They are all core tasks for the DBE. SSRS is really a reporting tool that is usually used by the reporting or data analyst.

Reason for question (3): The answers here should include how at least one of the tasks in the previous question was performed. For example, candidates should explain how they implemented replication or performance tuning and how this solved a business problem.

Reason for question (4): The answers here should include at least one feature (no matter how small) that the candidate has led from start to finish.

Reason for question (5): The answers here should tell you the pace of the candidate's current or past organization and what pace he or she is most comfortable with. Whether the frequency was once or twice a week or once a month, the answer should also highlight the candidate's preference for a fast-paced environment or for family time and some level of order.

Database Administrator (DBA)

The DBA's main focus is, as the title implies, the administration of the database—its availability, security, and accessibility, among other factors. The DBA's tasks revolve around planning, installation, configuration, backup, and maintenance of database servers in a production environment. He or she works with systems administrators to configure best-practice security and high-availability database systems and configuration managers, DevOps, and systems administrators to ensure that the most recent and tested code is propagated to the production environment. The DBA is most interested in the performance and optimization of database objects in the production environment.

Résumé Phrases, Database Administrator

Performed capacity planning for memory and space. Performed database consistency checks using DBCC stored procedures. Responsible for the installation, upgrade, and configuration of all company SQL Servers. Planned, executed, and maintained database installations, upgrades, service packs, security patches, and scheduled database tasks. Managed user accounts and assigned permissions. Performed replication and log shipping. Established and implemented database backup and recovery policies and practices. Monitored data and log file growth, disk utilization, memory, and CPU.

Keywords of note: optimization, log shipping, replication, mirroring, backup/recovery.

Figure 9.4. Phrases on a database administrator's résumé

Recruiter Conversation with a Database Administrator

The following are some questions a technical recruiter might ask database administrators to understand their experience level and fit.

The recruiter may start by going through the preliminaries of basic recruiter and candidate greetings and then flow right into the interview.

QUESTIONS

Greeting:
"Hi. My name is Helen Olive from ABC Solutions. I saw your résumé online and wanted to find out more about your skill sets in relation to a position I have today .... Is this okay?"

Interview:

"I'm going to ask you some general questions; your answers will give me a better understanding of what you do and perhaps what you enjoy the most in your job as a database administrator. Is that okay?"

(1) "Please describe your production database environment: how many database servers you administer, how many people are in your group, and who you report to."

(2) "What database technologies have been implemented in your environment—technologies such as mirroring, replication, snapshot, and log shipping? How do you use each of these technologies? If there's an issue/problem with any of these implemented technologies in your organization, how does it affect your organization?"

(3) "Is there a separation of tasks between database development and administration in your current/past organization? Do you find yourself doing the DBA as well as the DBE work? Which of these would you rather be doing?"

(4) "Regarding performance tuning, describe a performance issue that you helped resolve. What tools or combination of tools did you use?"

These questions are designed to reveal the experience level of the database administrator and match their experiences with the requirements of the hiring manager. The following are some reasons that motivate the questions.

Reason for question (1): The answer to this question will tell you a lot about the candidate's current environment. If it's a small one and your job description wants a person who has worked in a large database group, this might present a small problem. It becomes less of an issue when you understand why the hiring manager wants a DBA with large group experience. If there are no explanations and your candidate has all the other needed skills, the onus is on the recruiter to make the case that your candidate is a good fit.

The main differences between individuals with experience in large groups versus small groups is that the large-group candidate has experience working in silos and understands bureaucracy requirements, knows to get written permission for every major task, and can accept doing the same tasks every day with little frustration. The small-group candidate, on the other hand, knows little about bureaucracy and may require daily work challenges in order to stay with the company.

Reason for question (2): The answer to this question will give you a better understanding of the technologies used in the candidate's organization and the part played by the candidate in implementing these technologies. The second part of the question will also give you (the recruiter) information on the candidate's troubleshooting inclinations.

Reason for question (3): The answer to this question will let you know the direction and type of organization the candidate currently works in. These days, organizations separate the tasks of the DBA from those of the DBE. When organizations combine the two, it's a clear indication that it does not need a specialized administrator or developer.

The combination of skills is also an indication that the organization is probably not a software development company and rather is mostly charged with the maintenance of a database system that supports an internally used software application.

Reason for question (4): Performance tuning is a major skill requirement for most DBA work. Most DBAs with more than a year's experience may have encountered a performance issue at one time or another. You will profit by hearing about one such experience and the part the candidate played in resolving the issue.

Data Analyst

A data analyst is a combination of a business analyst and a report writer. The business analyst skills that come into play for the data analyst include (1) the ability to perform requirements gathering from business units in order to understand the kinds of information needed for decision-making, (2) the ability to work closely with different departments to define, develop, and deploy reports, (3) and a good understanding of the organization's business—how it works and the flow of information and finances.

Data analysts must understand the business of the organization in order to detect and analyze trends within data collected by the company. They must also have a keen understanding of relational database concepts and database structure. Knowledge of statistics may also be a major requirement for some organizations.

Résumé Phrases, Data Analyst

Trends analysis, data analysis, business requirements, scheduled report delivery, ad hoc reports, SQL Server Reporting Services (SSRS), Oracle reports, write SQL queries with SQL Server T-SQL or Oracle PL/SQL, data extraction, data transfer, and data load (using SSIS).

Keywords of note: trends, requirements, SQL, SSIS.

Figure 9.5. Phrases on a data analyst's résumé

Recruiter Conversation with a Data Analyst

Here are some questions a technical recruiter might ask data analysts to understand their experience level, analytic skills, and focus. The recruiter wants to know the database skills of the candidate.

The recruiter may start by going through the preliminaries of basic recruiter and candidate greetings and then flow right into the interview.

Greeting:

"Hi. My name is Helen Olive from ABC Solutions. I saw your résumé online and wanted to find out more about your skill sets in relation to a position I have today …. Is this okay?"

Interview:

"I'm going to ask you some general questions; your answers will give me a better understanding of what you do and perhaps what you enjoy the most in your job as a data analyst. Is that okay?"

(1) "Please describe your database reporting environment: how many reporting servers are available in your environment, the makeup of your team, and the platform you support."

(2) "How does your reporting environment get refreshed with current data from the production environment? Who in your team performs this task? Is the refresh task automated?"

(3) "Do you consider yourself a business data analyst or a data analyst? Why, in either case?"

(4) "What business trends have you identified in your database system? Can you describe one and the considerations that led you to conclude that this was a trend?"

(5) "Do you aspire to move from the role of data analyst to that of SQL developer in the future? Or have you worked as a SQL developer in the past?"

You may notice that the above questions are designed to reveal the experience level of the data analyst and match his or her experiences with the requirements of the hiring manager. The following are some reasons that motivate the questions.

Reason for question (1): The answer to this question brings to light the general data environment of the candidate, such as the number of servers, type of software, and the size of the data analyst team.

Reason for question (2): The answer to this question highlights the data analyst's understanding of the data environment. There may be three to four database environments in an organization, such as development, quality assurance, staging, production, and reporting/data warehouse environments. Data in the reporting and data warehouse environments comes from production. The process that leads to the flow of data from production to reporting is what the recruiter wants to make sure the data analyst understands and can articulate. Possible answers can include data replication, backup/restore, snapshot, and so forth.

Reason for question (3): The titles "business data analyst" and "data analyst" are sometimes synonymous. The former has the *business* prefix to suggest that the data analyst should have both business as well as technical inclinations.

Reason for question (4): The answer to this question draws attention to the candidate's experience and skill level. A data analyst candidate who describes trends in relation to their tasks and organization provides further confirmation of their experience.

Reason for question (5): This informs you about the candidate's SQL skill level. If the data analyst has never self-identified as a SQL developer, it may mean one of two things: first, it may indicate a strong affinity for the data analyst job because it combines business as well as technical knowledge but also an aversion to being considered only a technical person. Second, it may indicate the candidate's great confidence in his or her SQL skills to even be considering the more technical position. A data analyst with experience in creating stored procedures, functions, views, jobs, alerts, and so on will be very comfortable taking on a developer role. Of course, this opens up another dimension: whether this data analyst is really interested in data analysis. Since this was not the original reason this question was asked, we will focus on the reason that it was: to ascertain the level of the candidate's SQL skills. You are welcome to ask other follow-up questions that arise as a result of the candidate's answers.

ETL Developer

ETL developers are also known as data warehouse developers. Their main focus is on the migration, load, and integration of data into a data warehouse environment. They build database code that populates data from the production environment into the reporting and data warehouse environments. Using tools like SSIS, they perform all of the data transformations necessary to populate data into warehouse tables.

The ETL developer works with management and development teams to build business intelligence solutions. This person translates decision-support business requirements into technical design documents by creating data models that represent dataflow. These data models are developed bearing in mind the scalability and performance needs of a data warehouse system, an ever-expanding data repository.

The ETL developer creates ETL scripts and processes using SDLC. This person also reviews and tests all ETL scripts and processes (some organizations have an ETL tester as a separate job role). A big part of the ETL developer's job is to troubleshoot and tune the data warehouse and decision-support applications for optimal performance.

Résumé Phrases, ETL Developer

Data warehouse concepts and best practices, batch scripting, bulk insert operations in SQL Server, principles and techniques in data warehousing (OLAP, BI, metadata management, multidimensional database, data modeling, and cubes). Experience with data modeling and OLAP tools such as Erwin Data Modeler and Multidimensional Expressions (MDX). Experience in SSIS, SSRS, SQL Profiler, replication, Crystal Reports, TOAD, DBArtisian, ERwin.

Keywords of note: ETL, SSIS, DB modeling, OLAP, metadata, data warehouses.

Figure 9.6. Phrases on an ETL developer's résumé

Recruiter Conversation with an ETL Developer

These are some questions a technical recruiter might ask ETL developers to understand their experience level. The recruiter may start the conversation using the example below.

QUESTIONS

The recruiter may start by going through the preliminaries of basic recruiter and candidate greetings and then flow right into the interview.

Greeting:
"Hi. My name is Helen Olive from ABC Solutions. I saw your résumé online and wanted to find out more about your skill sets in relation to a position I have today …. Is this okay?"

Interview:

"I'm going to ask you some general questions; your answers will give me a better understanding of what you do and perhaps what you enjoy the most in your job as an ETL developer. Is that okay?"

(1) "Please describe your data warehouse environment: how many database servers you work with, how many people are in your group, and who you report to."

(2) "If your ETL process is documented, please describe what it entails. For instance, if there's new data to be extracted, transformed, and loaded into your database, how would you start this process while adhering to your documented processes?"

The above questions are designed to reveal the experience level of ETL developers and match their experiences with the requirements of the hiring manager. The following are some reasons that motivate the questions.

Reason for question (1): As with all the previous job roles, you want to understand the candidate's current work environment.

Reason for question (2): The answer to this question reveals if the candidate has followed a documented process for performing ETL processes, his or her understanding of this process, and whether the candidate was part of the process development. You will also gain more understanding of the considerations and process regarding ETL in the candidate's current organization.

Comparing Database Roles

Table 9.1 summarizes the data roles. A look at the different database roles in the table reveals how each role manipulates the same objects to fit its job function. Though the data analyst works with the same objects as the developer, he or she does so in a different capacity and for a different purpose. The different purposes define the design and data manipulation considerations of each role. Table 9.1 differentiates the database roles and can be used in managing the transition of candidates from one role to another.

	Database Engineer (DBE)	Database Administrator (DBA)	ETL Developer	Data (Report) Analyst
Overall Database	Designs database solutions using tables, stored procedures, functions, views, and indexes.	Maintenance of database systems in production environment.	Extracts data from one system, scrubs and transforms the data to fit destination table, and then loads that data.	Writes reports/ queries from data stored in tables.

Environment	Works in development and testing environments. These are internal non-customer-facing systems.	Works in production environment. This is an external customer-facing system.	Works in the data warehouse environment, an internal non-customer-facing system.	Works in the report environment, an internal non-customer-facing system.
Stored Procedures	Designs procedures that insert data into tables; updates or deletes data already in tables.	May write and execute procedures that perform database tuning and maintenance.	Creates stored procedures that automate the process of extracting, scrubbing, or loading data.	Writes procedures that "select" data stored in tables. Does not update or delete data he or she is reporting from.
Tables	Creates many tables to store data required for the solution at hand.	Maintains tables created by the DBE in the production environment.	Creates many tables to store data in between loads and in the data warehouse solution.	May create several tables to store subsets of data for analysis.
Performance Tuning	Optimizes and tunes database objects in order that they may perform better and faster.	Carries out any further optimization required in the production environment.	Optimizes database objects used in the ETL process.	Optimizes the database objects used in running reports.

Table 9.1. Database roles

A person whose primary function is administration cannot be confused with a developer or a data analyst; similarly, we have tried to differentiate the foci of these four positions so it becomes clearer to the technical recruiter what to look for when reviewing the résumés that come in for any of these positions.

There used to be a blurring of the tasks of the DBA and the DBE. Currently, given the highly specialized skill sets of either job, there is now minimal blurring of the two roles. That said, there are still some companies that maintain job descriptions that combine the skill sets of both the DBE and DBA. School districts or smaller companies are good examples of organizations that may not have the need for both a full-time DBA and a full-time DBE. This is because there isn't enough work to require these two positions. The solution is to have one person perform both tasks. Although some candidates can perform both, it's not generally an acceptable scenario.

What We Learned

- Database applications are built based on their need to perform either online transaction processing or online analytical processing—decision support.
- The official database language is SQL, declared to be a standard by ANSI in 1986.
- Database objects are the tangible components that make up a database. A few of them are as follows:
  - Tables, which contain rows and columns that store the attributes of an item
  - Stored procedures, which are programmatic objects that are executed automatically and are used to validate data, control database access, and return database results
  - Views, which are queries that act as filters to an underlying table

- Database administrators (DBAs) are different from database engineers (DBEs). The former are engaged in the administration of the production system, while the latter are developers/programmers and write code using database syntax.
- In looking more closely at database-related job descriptions, we analyzed the responsibilities and qualifications of the database developer and database administrator.
- We identified the main differences between the major database roles of the developer, administrator, analyst, and ETL developer.
- Each job role that was reviewed included the analysis of real-world job tasks and what the people in these roles take into consideration for their daily tasks.
- We reviewed a typical recruiter conversation with a database developer, database administrator, data analyst, and ETL developer.

CHAPTER 10

BIG DATA

In This Chapter

- What is big data?
- big data technologies
- traditional databases versus big data
- big data job roles
- the analysis of a big data job description

What Is Big Data?

The term *big data* is used to describe collections of data with large *volume*, great *variety*, and rapid *velocity*. Put another way, big data refers to data that is so big that traditional processes are not able to handle it. The explosive data growth that comes from the increased use of connected devices, internet services, and social media create big data. Big data became a hot topic in the late 2000s, and it has continued to grow in popularity. As our data footprint continues to grow in volume, variety, and velocity, the computing requirements necessary to store and analyze that data will also grow.

- *Volume.* This means that the amount or quantity of data is large. Volumes of data are created by social media (e.g., Twitter and Facebook) sensor data, the Internet of Things (IoT), web logs, and meter data.

- *Variety.* This means that the data has different formats. The data can be structured (organized) or nonstructured (disorganized). Structured data can come from business data that are already organized in database tables. Unstructured data can come from text messages, images, videos, photos, music, sound, and so on.

- *Velocity.* This means that data arrives at breakneck speeds. Streaming data, sensor data, traffic data, and weather data are examples of data that come with great speeds and sometimes in real time.

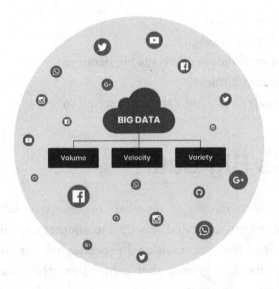

Figure 10.1: Big Data

Data growth creates two main challenges. The first challenge relates to the data storage capacity needed to capture, store, and analyze vast amounts of unstructured and structured data. Traditional database software and hardware are inefficient at handling the volume, velocity, and veracity of big data. The second challenge relates to the database technology needed to process and analyze the massive amount of data. Traditional relational database management systems (RDBMS) worked well for updating small amounts of data but fail when updating larger quantities of data. Furthermore, traditional database technologies required a predetermined data structure and were inefficient at managing the variety of data formats available with big data (e.g., XML, text, video, audio, emails, and sensor data).

Why Big Data Is Important

Big data can mean different things to different organizations. However, it means very little without the perspective of the value it creates for organizations. More data is created daily by billions of people and connected devices around the world. This data spans many industries: automotive, financial services, utility, and agriculture, to name a few.

If this data is captured and harnessed, it can become a great source of competitive advantage for organizations. Organizations that recognize the potential value that big data creates can begin to ask new questions about their businesses—questions that previously did not exist for the organization. A driver for creating value from big data is being able to analyze the data—that is, using analytics software to probe the data and derive new insights. Big data is of little value without analytics.

The Difference: Traditional Database Systems versus Big Data Systems

Traditional database technologies are used for managing data stored in *relational* databases (e.g., Oracle, Microsoft SQL Server, and MySQL).

A relational database organizes data based on the relational nature of the data.

Given that big data grows fast, moves fast, and is very diverse in form, traditional databases are not able to manage such data. Big data is usually stored using nonrelational database technologies (e.g., NoSQL, MongoDB).

Another difference between traditional databases and big data technologies is related to file read speeds (White 2012). Even though storage for traditional databases has become cheaper, the technology used for file reads has not evolved as fast. What this means is that it takes a long time for traditional database systems to read data from hard disks. This can be inefficient for big data, especially with the vast amounts of data that need to be read.

Compared to traditional databases, big data has also brought about paradigm and perspective shifts. According to IBM (2014), while the traditional approach is to analyze the data after it has been processed, the big data approach analyzes the data in motion—in real time. In addition, while the traditional approach seeks to carefully cleanse the data before it is analyzed, the big data approach seeks to analyze the data as is and then cleanse later if needed.

Differences	Traditional RDBMS	Big Data
Data storage	Relational	Nonrelational
Data analysis	Analyzes data after it has been processed and stored in a warehouse Analyzes small subsets of data	Analyze data in motion as it is generated in real time Analyzes all available data
Data cleansing	Cleanse and organize data before analysis	Analyze the data as is and then cleanse later if needed

File read	Slower reads and writes for large amounts of data	High-speed reads and writes
Assumption about data	Data analysts already know the questions they need to answer	Big data analysts will only identify the questions as they analyze the data

Table 10.1. Difference between traditional RDBMS and big data

Big Data Technologies and Applications

Challenges in storage and database technologies provided the impetus for big data technologies such as Hadoop. Hadoop is an open-source framework for processing, storing, and analyzing massive amounts of distributed data (Sharda et al. 2014). Another way to describe Hadoop is that it has a mechanism for processing large amounts of distributed data that are spread out across commodity (cheap) computers that have been configured to run as a cluster (Apache 2018). Currently an important part of the big data landscape, Hadoop is a project under the Apache Software Foundation and was originally created by Doug Cutting while working at Yahoo!

Hadoop has an interesting architecture, one that allows it to comb through and analyze vast amounts of data at significantly lower cost than traditional relational database systems. Hadoop has two primary functions: storing data and processing data. Storage is provided by the Hadoop Distributed File System (HDFS), and data processing is performed by MapReduce (White 2012).

Hadoop Ecosystem

Hadoop is best thought of as an ecosystem—that is, a network of interconnected systems. Therefore, as an ecosystem, Hadoop needs to have other systems that help support its functions. The Hadoop ecosystem consists of both open-source projects and commercially available applications. In addition to MapReduce, a few of those application systems are described below.

MapReduce

MapReduce is programming software for writing applications that process large amounts of data that reside on clusters of cheap (commodity) hardware. Its behavior is divided into three steps. First, it splits (maps) the input data into chunks. Second, it processes the data in a parallel manner and then sorts the outputs into a series of keys and values, placing same keys next to each other. The third step is the reducer, where all the values that have the same key are placed in a contiguous block. This type of processing increases performance, allowing for data to be easily split across many computers. Hadoop is usually used for running MapReduce, but many newer nonrelational database systems (e.g., MongoDB, NoSQL) also support MapReduce.

Apache Pig

Apache Pig is a scripting language for processing and analyzing large data sets in a Hadoop environment. Pig automates and reduces the complexity of MapReduce programming. Pig users can write complex MapReduce functions using Pig's simple scripting language called Pig Latin; Pig then automatically generates MapReduce functions. Popular languages like Java, Ruby, and Python are supported by Pig so that developers who are more familiar with those languages can write MapReduce functions using a language more familiar to them. What this means is that traditional developers can remain productive in a big data-Hadoop environment.

Apache Hive

A variant of SQL, Apache Hive is a standard for writing SQL queries in a Hadoop environment. Hive was developed as a language bridge between Hadoop and traditional database programs. Consequently, it provides a familiar database language that can be used instead of learning MapReduce. With Hive, developers can program Hadoop jobs and summarize, explore, and analyze large sets of data using SQL. Once again, this means that traditional database programmers can remain productive in a big data-Hadoop environment.

Apache Sqoop

Apache Sqoop is a tool for transferring data between the Hadoop Distributed File System (HDFS) and traditional relational databases. Sqoop can be described as the equivalent of the ETL process in the Hadoop environment; the difference is it transfers bulk data in a more efficient manner. Some of the traditional relational databases that Sqoop works with are Oracle, MSSQL, and Teradata.

Apache HBase

Apache HBase is an open-source, nonrelational (NoSQL), distributed database used for storing big data. When you think of all the limitations of traditional RDMSs for big data, HBase addresses all of them. It is nonrelational, provides real-time read and write access, and can store billions of rows of data and millions of columns of data. It can store combinations of a wide variety of data formats and structures. It is integrated with Hadoop, which allows it to take advantage of the Hadoop structure.

Big Data Analytics and Data Science

The value of big data is realized with analytics. Hence, big data and analytics are tightly connected. Even though big data is a relatively new concept, analytics is not. They are many analytics approaches that have been used in the past, such as machine learning, regression analysis, and text mining. However, the evolution of big data (volume, variety, and velocity) is changing the landscape of data analytics job roles. Today, job titles for individuals with skills and experience in both big data and data analytics include "big data analyst" or "data scientist."

Some may argue that the skill sets of the traditional data analyst are similar to those of big data analysts. Based on the previous discussions about the difference between the traditional RDMS and big data, one could argue that the skill sets and requirements actually differ.

The term *data science* is an old concept used to describe the combination of statistics, data analysis, machine learning, deep learning, mathematics, and artificial intelligence. As such, it represents an interdisciplinary approach to analyzing data in order to understand a phenomena and gain insight that is important for today's data explosion. Techniques and approaches used in data science come from the above-mentioned disciplines and include theory-driven hypothesis testing, data mining, text mining, machine learning, statistics, database management, and data visualization.

The term *data science* was initially used by Naur (1968), a scientist who wrote a paper on the science of data. Data science is sometimes known as data-driven science or the study of data (Longbing 2017), which means it uses scientific methods to analyze data.

In 2012, an article by Davenport and Patil (2012) in *Harvard Business Review* referred to data scientist as "the sexiest job of the 21st century."

The article helped propel the data scientist job role to new heights, establishing the demand for this type of talent. At the time, there were no clear definitions of what the job role really entailed. The role was one thing in one organization and another in the next. Whether it's "data analytics on steroids" or "statistics on steroids," the debate over what it is and should be continues (Longbing 2017).

At the time that article was published, there were few universities offering courses in data science, and it seemed difficult to break into the field. However, today, the initial rush for data science has waned, in part because many more universities are offering data science programs and some of the skill sets are seemingly not as difficult to acquire if one has access to the right tools. The one requirement that is still a little difficult and time-consuming to acquire is an advanced degree (e.g., a master's or PhD in statistics, mathematics, computer science, or information systems).

You might ask why hiring managers still require an advanced degree if the candidate has the desired experience and the skill sets. The answer is embedded in the definition of the term *data science*, which still represents an interdisciplinary approach that uses scientific methods, statistics, mathematics, and so on to analyze large amounts of data, make sense of them, and find actionable insights. These approaches are often learned and used as part of acquiring an advanced degree.

So, data science not only capitalizes on analyzing big data using open-source and commercially available tools but also employs myriad processes to understand the data.

In the following section, we describe two job roles—big data analyst and data scientist—and identify some differences technical recruiters should pay attention to.

Big Data Job Roles

Big Data Analyst

A big data analyst is a person who has hands-on experience with the Hadoop ecosystem (HDFS, MapReduce, Hive, Pig, Sqoop, Spark) and knows how to design a data ingestion and data processing architecture using data sources from traditional and big data sources such as Hadoop and Teradata. Such an analyst should also have experience using ETL tools in a Hadoop environment (e.g., Pentaho). This person has many years of experience as a data analyst, database engineer, or software engineer in a large organization and typically has some advanced-level database programming skill set in traditional relational database environments. A big data analyst also needs to know how to represent data visually using common visualization tools.

Requirements
- Bachelor's or master's degree in computer science, information systems, or related field
- 5+ years' experience in enterprise data environments
- 5 years of experience using R, Python, and Scala in a Hadoop environment
- Experience developing ETL processes using SQL, Pig, HIVE, Python, and Shell scripting
- Experience with data visualization tools (e.g., Tableau, Qlikview)

Data Scientist

A data scientist has demonstrated experience applying data modeling, scientific methods, and statistical concepts to large data sets. This person has an advanced technical degree in data science, applied computer science concepts, or applied mathematics. He or she has demonstrable experience using advanced statistical analysis programs such as SAS, SPSS, R, and STATA and performing advanced parametric and nonparametric statistical analyses. A data scientist is also able to structure data using multiple techniques, writing algorithms, and programming languages such as Java and Python.

Requirements
- Master's or PhD in computer science, statistics, or related quantitative field
- 5 years' experience in data science
- Experience working with data analysis methodologies, statistics, text mining
- Experience working with statistics programs such as SAS, SPSS, and STATA
- Experience creating statistical models and performing quantitative analyses (e.g., regression, decision trees)
- Experience with MapReduce, R, Java, and Python
- Experience working with data on HDFS, Cassandra, and MongoDB

Difference between Data Scientist and Big Data Analyst

After sampling job roles on the major technical job sites (e.g., Dice, Indeed), some differences in how the data scientist and big data analyst are described and in their job requirements became clear. Some of the differences between the job role descriptions and requirements are highlighted in table 10.2.

There is a difference in the education requirement for a data scientist and a big data analyst for the reasons mentioned earlier. Data scientist roles require a PhD or master's degree versus the requirement of a bachelor's or master's for big data roles. There are also differences in the quantitative, visualization, and reporting experience requirements. For data scientist roles, there are requirements for statistics-based analyses but not so much for big data analyst roles. Furthermore, there are few or no requirements for visualization or reporting for data scientists, whereas big data roles do require skills in these areas.

	Data Scientist	Big Data Analyst
Education requirement	PhD or master's degree in computer science, engineering, or related quantitative fields	Bachelor's or master's degree in computer science, engineering, or related fields
Quantitative experience	Statistics based in logistic regression, decision trees, data and text mining, machine learning	When quantitative experience is requested, it is usually as a "nice to have"
Visualization experience	Usually not a requirement	Some emphasis on visualization
Reporting experience	Usually not a requirement	Some emphasis on reporting using traditional databases

Table 10.2. Job role differences between data scientist and big data analyst

The Big Data Analyst Job Description

The big data analyst's job is primarily to analyze vast amounts of data for the purpose of extracting insights for businesses. Therefore, analysts spend their time working in the Hadoop ecosystem using the tools available in that environment to move data between Hadoop-based databases (e.g., NoSQL, HBase) and traditional databases (e.g., SQL Server, Teradata), analyze the data, and then represent the data using visualization tools.

Responsibilities

(1) Design and implement data processing of large datasets in a <u>Hadoop environment</u>

(2) <u>Work closely with other big data, reporting</u>, and analytics team members

(3) <u>Load data (ETL)</u> from a variety of relational and nonrelational sources into the big data environment

(4) Work with structured and unstructured data processes

(5) Transform big data into <u>graphical representations</u> that facilitate insights

Requirements

(1) Bachelor's or master's degree in computer science or a related field

(2) 3+ years of hands-on experience in big data environments (Hadoop/ HDFS, Spark, HBase, Pig, Hive, Scala)

(3) 5+ years of experience in a database engineer or data analytics role

(4) Experience working with data visualization tools

(5) Advanced experience in SQL programming in relational and NoSQL databases

Figure 10.2. Sample job description for a big data analyst

Responsibilities and Requirements Analysis

Hadoop environment. Since this is a big data position, the analyst must be very familiar with Hadoop and how data processing works in a distributed data environment. This environment and its tools are a little different from the traditional database tools. As mentioned earlier, big data varies with different organizations. What might be considered big data in one organization might be "tiny" in others. Hence, it might be useful for the recruiter to directly ask about the size of the datasets at play in the organization.

Work closely with other big data and reporting team members. Although the job title may say big data analyst, the job description might be a little closer to a data analyst or reporting analyst position. If that's the case, the recruiter should ask more questions to ascertain if this is a data analyst who works in a big data environment. It is quite possible that a traditional data analyst may work in a big data environment but only work with a subset of the data.

Load data (ETL) from a variety of relational and nonrelational sources. The big data analyst must have experience working with datasets from different sources, including traditional relational databases such as SQL, Oracle, and Teradata and nonrelational databases such as MongoDB, NoSQL, and HBase. These data sources are usually spelled out in the job description. If they are not, the recruiter should ask questions to find out more. The Hadoop environment supports several ETL tools for extracting, transforming, and loading data to and from relational and nonrelational databases (e.g., Sqoop). The analyst should be familiar with a few of the ETL tools in the Hadoop environment, especially the open-source versions. ETL processes are straightforward once you have a good understanding of the source and destination of the data.

Graphical representations / data visualization tools. Since the value derived from big data is the insights business leaders gain from the data, it is imperative that these insights be presented in a way that makes them easy to grasp. Visualization tools are used to present these insights in graphical formats that are easy for decision makers to read. This is another instance where the job description bears more of a resemblance to data visualization than it does to big data analytics, thus presenting another opportunity for the recruiter to ask questions to find out more. It might be both, in which case it is beneficial for the recruiter to understand the proportion of data visualization versus big data analytics. For example, is the position 60 percent visualization and 40 percent big data analytics?

Database engineer or data analytics role / SQL programming. A big data analyst needs strong skills in database programming. This position calls for advanced experience as a database developer. The skill set of a database developer is easily transferable to a big data analyst role. This is mostly because some of the data tools in the Hadoop environment were created to allow the transfer of those skills and to reduce the learning curve in the Hadoop environment. For example, Apache Hive and Apache Pig are Hadoop ecosystem applications for which a developer's SQL skills come in very handy.

Questions for the Candidate

Now that you understand the role of the big data analyst, the following are sample questions that you might ask your candidate to further understand their experience and skills and explanations of the purpose of the questions. These questions will help the recruiter evaluate the candidate's fit with the job description.

QUESTIONS

- "Could you please describe your experience designing database models in a big data environment?"
    o You learn about the candidate's general experience working in this environment and some of the tools they have used.
- "What are some common issues you have encountered with working in a big data/Hadoop environment?"
    o This is a general question that provides insight into the candidate's overall experience in the Hadoop environment. There are almost always issues dealing with data. A response of "no issues" is not an ideal one.
- "How has your previous experience (as a SQL developer, Java developer, etc.) helped you as a big data analyst?"
    o With this question, you are assuming that your candidate has some prior experience as a SQL developer. This is a good assumption. If you recall, the foundation of big data is data. It also tells you that the candidate's experience surpasses the level of "Learn Hadoop in Six Months on Your Own," not that there is anything wrong with that. However, there's more to working with data, especially if the job description requires strong SQL experience.

- "How much of your current work calls for using quantitative or statistical processes such as regression, decision trees, or structural equation modeling to analyze data?"
  - o Although quantitative analysis is usually a strongly desired skill, it is not required in most big data analyst positions. Nonetheless, it would be beneficial to know the extent of your candidate's skills. Experience in this area might make them more appealing to the hiring manager. It could also be the skill you need for another position.
  - o If the candidate does not volunteer the tools he or she used for running quantitative analyses, definitely ask them (e.g., SPSS, SAS, Stata, Minitab, R).
- "How much of the data analysis you carried out required specifying a hypothesis beforehand?"
  - o This question can also be used as a follow-up to the previous question or as a stand-alone. As a follow-up question, it is designed to obtain a better understanding of the candidate's level of expertise in quantitative analysis using statistical tools. If he or she has some experience, the answers might be lengthy! The answer might include a description of the questions for which answers were being sought and perhaps why these were considered questions that needed answers. If there were questions or hypotheses beforehand, it may be an indication that the task was essentially data analysis and not necessarily big data analysis. If you recall, the questions are not usually known in advance with big data.
  - o If this is a stand-alone question, the response will indicate the candidate's level of expertise in data analysis methods.

What We Learned

- Big data is used to describe collections of data of large volume, great variety, and rapid velocity. Volume means that the amount or quantity of data is large. Variety means that there are different types or formats of data. Velocity means that data is arriving at breakneck speeds.

- Data growth creates two main challenges: the first is the data storage capacity needed to capture, store, and analyze the data; the second is the database technology needed to process and analyze the massive quantities of data.
- A driver for creating value from big data is being able to analyze the data.
- There is an important difference between traditional database systems and big data systems. Traditional database technologies are used for managing data stored in relational databases (e.g., Oracle, Microsoft SQL Server). Big data is usually managed with nonrelational databases technologies (e.g., NoSQL, MongoDB).
- Hadoop is an open-source framework for processing, storing, and analyzing massive amounts of distributed data. Hadoop has two primary functions: storing data and processing data. Storage is provided by HDFS, and data processing and analysis is performed by MapReduce.
- Data science is a term used to describe a combination of statistics, data analysis, machine learning, deep learning, mathematics, and artificial intelligence. Data science is sometimes known as data-driven science or the study of data.

CHAPTER 11

INFORMATION SECURITY

In This Chapter

- overview of information security
- goal of information security
- security threats, vulnerabilities, and attacks
- information security technologies
- information security job roles

Overview of Information Security

The dictionary definition of *security* is "the state of being secure and free from danger or harm" (*Merriam-Webster*). Information security started with computer security. Computer security is the protection of computer systems and the data they house from theft, damage, or disruption. Computer security is not new. In the early days, computer security focused more on the security of the physical machine. The advent of networking and the internet has changed the way computer and information security are viewed and addressed. When computers were stand-alone devices with little or no connectivity or networking with other devices, information security was less of a problem. Think about it for a second: if you cannot get to a computer, then how can it be compromised by a remotely located person through a network or the internet? The concern then was about the physical security of computers from theft and damage and not necessarily information security.

According to the Committee on National Security Systems (CNSS), information security is the protection of information and its critical elements, including the systems and hardware that use, store, and transmit that information. The difference between computer security and information security lies in the scope of the protection. Whereas computer security is confined to the protection of the computer system and the data it houses, information security encompasses the protection of hardware, software, data, people, processes, and networks.

Information security refers to the practice of preventing, detecting, and recovering from incidences of unauthorized disclosure, use, access, disruption, or modification of information. The prevention, detection, and recovery are performed across all information and systems, whether they are end systems (operating systems, files, databases, logs, etc.) or systems in transit (e-commerce, banking, file transfers, emails, etc.).

Information assurance is the basis for confidence that security measures, both technical and operational, will work as intended to protect the system and the information it processes (NIST 2014)

Basic Concepts of Information Security

Information systems consist of many components that need to be properly secured, including hardware, software, data, procedures, and people. The basics of information systems security refer to the protection of hardware, software, data, procedures, and people in terms of three goals: *confidentiality, integrity,* and *availability* (CIA). See figure 11.1. How these three goals are viewed depends on the environment, context, needs of the organization, and the law (Bishop 2007).

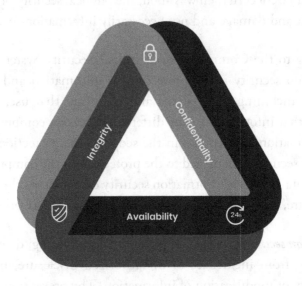

Figure 11.1. Information security concepts.

Confidentiality

In the simplest terms, *confidentiality* is the hiding of information. To develop that idea a bit more, confidentiality is the hiding of information and making it available only to authorized persons or systems that need to know the information. From an individual's perspective, it is the requirement to keep a person's private information restricted to only authorized users and for authorized uses. The types of information that a person could want kept confidential include health care and financial information. From an organization's perspective, proprietary and intellectual property are elements that may be subject to confidentiality restrictions for obvious reasons.

Organizations may not want their secret formula to be readily available for their competitors to see. Confidentiality ensures that only authorized humans and systems are able to access certain information. Confidentiality of information systems is threatened when unauthorized persons or systems can access information without correct authorization. For example, your confidentiality is breached when an unfamiliar person (not a relative, your doctor, or your health care provider) can view or access your medical or financial records.

Integrity

Honesty, truthfulness, and *veracity* are all synonyms of *integrity.* Integrity in information security refers to the quality of being unaltered, uncorrupted, and whole. For the purposes of information security, the notion of information integrity deals with (1) whether one can trust the content of information and (2) whether one can trust the source or origin of information (Bishop 2007). If either of these is compromised, the information lacks integrity. An example might be when a person presents information from a book and cites the author correctly (origin) but alters the information in a manner inconsistent with the author's purpose (content). The information in this case has *origin integrity* but lacks *content integrity* (Bishop 2007). Therefore, the information does not have integrity. Integrity can also be compromised when an individual's information is altered without his or her knowledge. When grades are altered in a grading software system, the source has integrity, but the content does not. The goal of information security is to prevent such alterations through preventing and detecting attempts to compromise integrity.

Availability

Availability in information security is the requirement for information to be accessible to the user when it is needed and without delays. When information (e.g., an applicant tracking system) is not accessible for a recruiter to do their job, availability becomes an issue. Given the possibility that certain individuals might deliberately render a system and its information unavailable by denying others access to it, availability becomes an important factor in information security.

Denial of service (DoS) is a mechanism often used by attackers to compromise availability. DoS is a type of cyberattack by which a hacker renders a system, its information, or its services unavailable to its users by deliberately disrupting its normal working condition. Availability can be compromised when attackers flood the target systems with traffic or cause the system to crash. In both cases, the system is unavailable to its users until the disruption is resolved.

Goal of Information Security

The increase in high-profile security breaches and the impact of such breaches on the victimized organizations have become key concerns for organizations and their stakeholders. Organizations are finding that information security is no longer just a technology issue but also a management issue. As organizations grapple with addressing information security, the overall goal is to protect the confidentiality, integrity, and availability of information system resources.

Although the overall goal of information security is highly important, it is a very broad one that casts a wide net and that can sometimes seem vague. Hence, there is more to achieving the goals of information security than just focusing on confidentiality, integrity, and security (CIA). In the following sections, you will learn about information security threats, vulnerabilities, and attacks and how they can be prevented and blocked. In cases where they cannot be prevented or blocked, the impact on organizations is severe. For example, the security breaches that affected organizations such as Home Depot, Target, Anthem, and Sony compromised more than two hundred million records. These organizations were impacted through loss of business, reputation, customer churn, and legal fees, and some of them were sued.

Fortunately, there are information security technologies available to help organizations prevent and block these threats. Given that these technologies can be expensive to implement and support and can affect productivity, a challenge for organizations is to find the right balance of information security technologies and procedures that support the organization's overall strategic goal. Hence, though the overall goal of information security is CIA, this goal can be further nuanced for each organization as it considers how the technologies that support CIA can be applied within its business.

Security Threats, Vulnerabilities, and Attacks

Cybercriminals can attack our computers and information systems by compromising any of the three goals of information security: confidentiality, integrity, and availability. Now, let's delve into the threats, vulnerabilities, attacks, and safeguards of information security.

- A *threat* is a potential violation of security; that is, it's a potential for an event, incident, or circumstance that can have an adverse effect on an information system. A violation does not need to occur for an event to be considered a threat. The fact that the violation might occur makes it a threat.
- A *vulnerability* is a weakness in an information system that can be attacked. In other words, a vulnerability refers to a flaw or hole in software or hardware systems that creates an opportunity for an attacker to compromise a system's confidentiality, integrity, or availability.
- An *attack* is an actual violation of security. An attack occurs when a vulnerability is successfully exploited.

Figure 11.2. Vulnerability progression

Combining these terms, a flaw (vulnerability) that is neither identified nor addressed will increase the potential for an incident that can have an adverse effect a system (threat) and lead to an actual violation of the system's security (attack). Figure 11.2 depicts the progression from vulnerability, threat, and attack.

There will always be threats. However, it is more important that organizations focus on identifying and addressing vulnerabilities that can be exploited by attackers. Using home and car security as illustrations, there will always be threats of home and car burglaries. The vulnerabilities of a home or car include unlocked doors, open windows, and a lack of burglar or antitheft alarms. With these unaddressed vulnerabilities, the threat of burglary increases. However, the threat is reduced when the owner of the home or car identifies and closes off these vulnerabilities by applying locks, closing their windows at night, and installing alarms. Similarly, to address threats in an information security landscape, security professionals must identity and address vulnerabilities and flaws in their information systems to reduce security threats.

Safeguards are countermeasures that are put in place by individuals and organizations to avoid, prevent, react to, and recover from the effects of the threat. The sources of threats fall into three main categories: cybercrime, force of nature, and human errors.

Cybercrime threat is a potential for criminal activities that are performed using computers and the internet with the intent to disrupt, destroy, or damage information systems. Examples of cybercrime are password attacks, phishing, and hacking.

Force of nature present serious threats since they can happen without any prior notice. Examples of force of nature threats are fire, earthquakes, and floods. These may not only disrupt information systems but can also destroy human lives. Since it is difficult to avoid or prevent these types of threats, organizations use controls such as business continuity and disaster recovery to reduce the severity of damage.

Human error threat is a potential for individuals to unintentionally or ignorantly perform actions that damage or disrupt information systems. Employees can erroneously perform such actions when they lack adequate training or are ignorant of the organization's security policies. Employees are known to be the greatest source of security threats. Security training and awareness programs can help reduce this type of threat. Table 11.1 depicts the main categories and examples that fall under them.

	Cybercrime	**Force of Nature**	**Human Error**
Threat	Password attacks, malware, hacking, phishing, social engineering	Earthquakes, tornadoes, flood, fire	Accidental information disclosure and disposal

Table 11.1. Threat categories

Types of Attacks

Denial of Service Attack

A denial of service (DoS) attack is a type of attack that occurs when an attacker attempts to make information systems or network resources unavailable to its intended users by disrupting its services. The way a DoS typically works is that an attacker floods an internet-connected machine with so much traffic that it overwhelms the machine and limits its availability to serve its real users. A common symptom of an ongoing DoS attack on a website is when users are not able to access the website.

Web-Based Attack

A web-based attack is a type of attack that uses software programs to exploit vulnerabilities in web applications and websites, creating a path to a user's computer. Cross-site scripting (XSS) is a type of web-based attack and one of the most prevalent of web-based attacks. In an XSS attack, a web vulnerability is exploited to inject malicious code into a trusted website. An attacker uses a web application to send the malicious code in the form of a browser script.

There are many vulnerabilities that allow XSS attacks to occur. The vulnerability occurs when a web application uses input provided by a user (e.g., input entered on a web form) as part of its generated output without first validating or encoding the input. In other words, the web application uses untrusted input in its processes.

There are many ways to prevent XSS attacks. A number of prevention strategies have been included here so that you can recognize them in discussions with candidates. According to OWASP, the first rule to preventing XSS attacks is *never* to insert untrusted data, except in allowed locations. That is, untrusted data is not to be included in an HTML document. The second rule is to use HTML escape before inserting untrusted data into HTML content. This means that in situations where one must add untrusted data in HTML, one must at the very least use HTML escape characters. There are many more security rules involving using URL encoding, HTML validation, CSS encoding, and so on.

Social Engineering (Phishing)

Social engineering is the psychological manipulation of people into performing actions or disclosing confidential information. *Phishing* is a social engineering technique designed to fraudulently obtain confidential information from individuals. Attackers use emails to trick individuals into revealing information.

The messages in phishing emails are designed to draw the victim's interest or to induce a sense of urgency by asking the user to perform a task requiring them to reveal personal information. The main objective of the email message is to deceive the individual into thinking that it is from a trusted source.

Man-in-the-Middle Attack

When users initiate a transaction with a website, it creates a session between the individual's computer and the website's remote server. The session usually has a unique identification (ID) code, which should be private and known only to the individual's computer and the remote server. A man-in-the-middle attack occurs when someone comes between the individual's computer and the remote server and starts to actively monitor, capture, and intercept the communications between the systems. In a man-in-the-middle attack, the attacker hijacks the session by capturing the session ID and then uses it to pretend to be the victim's computer. The attacker is then able to make requests of the remote server under false pretenses.

Information Security Technologies and Procedures

This section describes the security technologies that help organizations prevent, detect, and recover from attacks. Some of the technology processes are firewalls, cryptography, intrusion prevention and detection systems, identity and authentication management, malware protection, application design, and vulnerability testing. It should be noted that security of information systems is never 100 percent guaranteed, even after installing all available security technologies.

Firewalls

A *firewall* is a combination of hardware and software systems that prevent unauthorized access to networks. It acts as a filter and checks incoming and outgoing traffic to ensure that only authorized traffic is allowed in or out. There are different types of firewalls that perform different functions. Each organization and its information security professionals decide how to configure and combine the different types to implement the functions they desire.

Cryptography

Cryptography is the art of creating and using codes to secure information. Cryptography originates from Greek words *krypto* and *graphein*, which translate to "hidden" and "to write." Encryption is a cryptographic process that transforms clear text into scrambled coded text for secure transmission and storage, in such a way that it is incomprehensible and cannot be used by unauthorized individuals or processes. When used in information security, encryption converts clear text to encoded text, while decryption unscrambles the encoded text back to its original clear text.

Organizations use encryption to convert sensitive information, such as your password, social security number, and credit card numbers, for storage. When sensitive information is transmitted over the internet, organizations use encryption protocols such as Secure Sockets Layer (SSL) and Transport Layer Security (TLS) to secure the transmission.

Intrusion Detection and Prevention Systems (IDPS)

IDPS is an information system that automatically *detects* an intrusion (an attacker's attempt to break into a system) and then changes its configuration to *prevent* an intrusion from successfully attacking its systems. IDPS is used primarily for (1) detecting intruders, (2) collecting information about the intrusion so that organizations can learn from it and prevent further intrusions, and (3) deterring intruders who are aware that an IDPS is deployed. This latter function acts in the same way a burglar alarm does, by deterring burglars.

Identity and Authentication Management (IAM)

IAM is an access control mechanism that determines if, how, when, from where, and the extent to grant access to an individual into an information system or a physical location. IAM uses a combination of technologies and policies to determine access. It relies on two main functions to determine an individual's access to permission and privileges: *identification* and *authentication*. Information systems require users to identify themselves using an identifier such as a username (identification) and to validate that they are authorized to use a system by using something they know, such as a password (authentication). Because usernames and passwords are very vulnerable to compromise, many organizations use more advanced IAM techniques, such as biometrics and multifactor authentication.

Malware Protection

Malware means malicious software and is a term used to describe a broad range of malicious programs and code that are used for disrupting, destroying, or damaging information systems. Examples of malware include viruses, Trojan horses, spyware, ransomware, and worms that infect systems and cause them to function in ways they were not originally meant to perform. Malware can delete files, block access to files, log user actions, control systems, and reconfigure systems, or self-propagate, all the while hiding or evolving to hide from being recognized. Organizations deploy and use malware protection (antimalware) programs to identify, delete, and prevent malware from operating. Since malware patterns can evolve to hide from being identified, organizations and their security professionals must constantly update their malware protection programs to identify changes in malware patterns.

Application Design and Security

Developers are encouraged to use application design principles to support and increase the security of their software. Application security principles are sets of recommended properties and implementation practices that reduce the risk (likelihood and severity) of a security threat to software. Using specific application design principles is important for supporting security. Traditionally, there are eight principles, but we highlight only two of them below.

- *The principle of least privilege* states that a subject should be given only the privileges needed to accomplish its tasks. If a subject does not need an access right, the subject should not be given that right.
- *The principle of complete mediation* calls for all access to objects to be checked to ensure that they are allowed. In practice, this principle is followed by using layered mechanisms to increase security in an application. Even though one layer of control may seem reasonable, more than one should be used to increase the difficultly of breaking the system.

Security and Vulnerability Testing

Security and vulnerability testing is a process for identifying and documenting specific flaws and vulnerabilities in an organization's information systems environment. Penetration testing is a type of vulnerability testing, it is a legal and authorized attempt to successfully identify and exploit vulnerabilities in information systems and networks to make the systems more secure. Such testing evaluates the strengths and weaknesses of all security controls on systems by intentionally violating security policies.

Even though organizations perform penetration tests periodically to test the system environments and identify vulnerabilities, penetration testing does not usually prove the absence of vulnerabilities. However, organizations can use one of two penetration testing methods to identify vulnerabilities: black-box or white-box pen testing. Black-box testing is when the tester has no prior knowledge of the configuration of the system and must violate its security policies, whereas white-box testing is when the tester has been given specific information about the systems to test and then seeks to increase unauthorized access (i.e., privilege escalation).

The Information Security Function (Organization Chart)

The information security organization is multifaceted, spanning and sometimes overlapping with traditional IT roles and management functions, such as those exercised by the CIO. Figure 11.3 depicts the information security organization chart with the chief information security officer (CISO) at the top. The function of the CISO may mean different things in different organizations, as they must base the CISO function on their needs, size, and organization structure. It should be noted that the functions of the CIO and CISO are different. The CIO's focus is usually on information technology operations and business management, which is more of an internal focus. On the other hand, the CISO's focus is usually on information security risk management, which is both internally and externally focused. According to the Software Engineering Institute (SEI), the office of the CISO is made up of four departments: security engineering, security operations, emergency and incident management, and program management. The next section follows the SEI CISO roadmap to describe each department and their subdepartments.

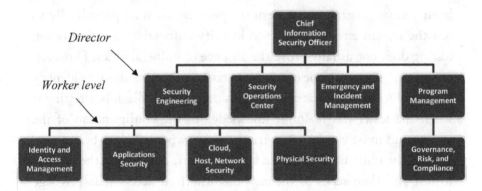

Figure 11.3. The Information Security Organization (Source: Software Engineering Institute)

The *security engineering* department is responsible for specifying the confidentiality, integrity, and availability requirements in the organization. They provide and maintain the organization's security architecture, technical benchmarks, the integration of security in software development lifecycles, and software configuration management in the organization. The four subdepartments housed under the security engineering department include identity management; application security; cloud, host, and network security; and physical security. Those four subdepartments are described below.

- o **Identity management.** Also known as access and identity management (AIM), it is a function that manages how users log in to systems (identity) and the resources users can access (access control) in the organization. The function depends on security policies to manage identities and control access to resources. It uses processes like biometrics, multifactor authentication, password management, and single sign-on to manage AIM.
- o **Application security.** This function oversees the inventory of all the organizations' software (e.g., operating systems, database systems, web applications). It also creates control mechanisms

that protect all software systems and oversees how software is configured (software configuration) and changed (change management) in the organization.

o **Cloud, host, and network security.** This function oversees the maintenance of all network and hardware devices. It creates, implements, and manages control mechanisms that protect all network and hardware systems. It uses processes like firewalls and intrusion prevention and detection systems to perform its duties.

o **Physical security.** This function oversees the inventory of all asset and facility security. It uses processes like encryption, backups, and data retention to maintain and control physical security and assets.

The security operations center (SOC) is tasked with performing real-time operational activities of securing the organization's information security resources. Their activities entail managing the processes for preventing, detecting, examining, and eliminating malware at the enterprise level. This function also maintains a system that gathers, analyzes, and reports malware (threat management system). This is where all monitoring and logging happens. This function monitors and logs all employee activities. Yes, this happens! It also monitors and logs activities from applications, networks, and access to all systems. This function uses firewalls, intrusion detection and prevention systems, and security event management systems to support the organization's security. This function also manages the organization's security help desk, which processes security incidents.

The emergency and incident management department is responsible for responding to and recovering from security incidents that are potentially severe to the organization's systems. Their primary responsibility is to respond to and recover from severe security incidents in a timely manner. Although their function overlaps with that of the SOC, they differ in the scope of their activities. This function handles business continuity planning, IT disaster recovery, and is responsible for performing a more extensive analysis of security incidents to gain a better understanding of how to prevent them in the future. To this end, they perform activities such as root cause analysis, forensic investigations, and vulnerability testing.

The program and project management department is responsible for creating an information security plan and implementing the plan across the organization. The governance, compliance, and risk management department is housed under the program and project management department.

- o **Governance, compliance, and risk management**. This function includes two subfunctions. First, the risk management subfunction creates the information security risk strategy for the organization. Second, the governance and compliance subfunction is the enforcement arm of the group. They enforce the information security program to ensure that it fulfils all security requirements pertaining to regulations, the law, policy, standards, and guidelines. Examples of such requirements are HIPAA and SOX.

Information Security Job Roles

Based on the previous section, which describes the information security functions, the section below describes the job roles that fit into those functions.

Chief Information Security Officer (CISO)

The CISO defines and improves the organization's information security risk strategy, ensuring that the InfoSec risk strategy aligns with the organization's strategy. Specifically, the CISO defines risk measurement standards and frameworks for each of the four security components (security engineering, security operations center, emergency and incident response management, and program management). In addition, the CISO develops and maintains the security policy, interfaces with both internal and external organizations (e.g., government regulators, vendors, media), and presents to the organization's board members. The CISO has expert knowledge in risk-management frameworks and regulations such as HIPAA, SOX, PCI, NIST, and HITRUST.

Responsibilities

- o Develops and maintains an information security governance, risk, and compliance program.
- o Measures and drives the governance, risk, and compliance program, including partnering with stakeholders to ensure compliance with standards such as PCI, HIPAA ISO, NIST, and COBIT. Ensures all compliance activities are mapped to defined standards.
- o Manages a security training and awareness program to drive and expand organizational security awareness across the organization.
- o Manages multiple teams in the design, development, delivery, and support of several critical security-related projects as part of maturing the organization's security capabilities.
- o Defines, develops, and manages the organization's security operations function. Manages both the day-to-day internal security organization and third-party security service providers for external network monitoring. Works with external entities regarding current threats, indicators of compromise, or other intelligence.
- o Defines metrics for, monitors, and measures incident-handling performance. Reports on the efficiency and effectiveness of security programs.
- o Acts as primary interface to audit organizations, including review of all IT-related audit findings, follow-ups, and management responses.

Core Requirements: Education, Experience, and Skills

- Degree in computer science, engineering, or information systems
- 10+ years of combined experience in risk management, information security, and IT
- 5+ years of experience in a senior leadership role (CISO or equivalent)
- Experience engaging with CIO/COO
- Experience working across several units to build an integrated IT security and risk strategy
- Experience designing and maintaining an enterprise-wide security architecture and infrastructure
- Experience managing complex project plans with interdependencies with other projects
- Experience working with external cyber intelligence organizations, such as ISACs, DHS, and the FBI
- Familiarity with standard risk frameworks such as NIST, PCI, HIPAA, ISO, and SANS frameworks
- Certified with CISSP, CISA, or equivalent other

Information Security Program Manager

The information security project manager is responsible for overall direction and support of information security projects in the organization. The security project manager ensures that project teams meet planned milestones and goals and engages in operational and strategic information security strategies. He or she develops and implements standardized security delivery in areas such as incidence response and incidence reporting as well as manages and tracks security projects to ensure that policies, processes, and procedures comply with standard security frameworks and best practices (e.g., NIST, PCI, HIPAA, and ISO).

Responsibilities
- Manages the initiation, planning, execution, and maintenance of information security programs
- Applies project management, resource management, budget management, risk management, and continuous security audits to information security projects
- Manages operational and strategic information security projects
- Uses PMO best practices in the development and maintenance of project artifacts
- Works with senior management to prioritize information security goals, objectives, and projects
- Manages the information-security and risk-management portfolio and ensures performance metrics are monitored and appraised
- Continuously identifies project risks and mitigation plans to minimize impact

Core Requirements
- 3+ years of experience in project management
- 1 year of experience in information security
- Familiarity and (or) experience managing projects such as cloud migration, data loss prevention, identity and access management
- Experience with risk management, change management, configuration management
- Experience with governance and compliance methodologies

Information Security Risk Analyst

This position is usually located in the project management office and specifically in the risk management team. The project management office defines the organization's security standards, performs risk assessments and planning, and measures organizational security performance. The information security risk analyst is responsible for managing information security risk for the organization. This person performs risk analysis and determines risk acceptance, risk avoidance, risk mitigation, or risk transfer in accordance with the organization's risk-management strategy. He or she has technical knowledge and (or) experience in security, networking, systems administration, database administration, and architecture processes and procedures. The information security risk analyst manages security policy, standards, and best practices that align with the organization's goals and protect the confidentiality, integrity, and availability of information systems.

Responsibilities
- Works with multiple business units to develop an overall risk-management strategy for existing and new services in accordance with established standards
- Works with the emergency and incidence response management group to assess the adequacy of business continuity and disaster recovery controls
- Works with the SOC to evaluate threats and vulnerabilities and then performs risk analysis, calculates the residual risk, and communicates risk-assessment findings to business units and senior management
- Ensures adherence and compliance to all applicable federal and state laws, regulations, and guidance (e.g., SOX, PCI, HIPAA, HITECH, USA Patriot Act)
- Contributes to creating organizational security policies, practices, standards, and procedures to protect the security of information system assets
- Assists project teams in the planning and implementation of security measures to comply with the organization's security policies and external regulations

Core Requirements:
- Degree in computer science, engineering, or information systems
- 5+ years of experience in information technology

- 3+ years of experience in information security risk management and governance programs
- Experience with and/or knowledge of networking and systems administration processes and tools (e.g., LAN/WAN, VPNs, firewalls, IDS/IPS)
- Experience evaluating evolving risks inherent in new technologies spanning networks
- Communication and presentation skills for interfacing with top management
- Experience in classifying security threats and performing vulnerability assessments
- Information security certification (e.g., CISSP, CISA, CISM, GIAC, or equivalent)
- Certified Risk and Information Systems Control (CRISC) or GRC Professional (GRCP)
- Experience with regulatory and compliance initiatives (e.g., HIPAA, NIST, HITECH, PCI, SOX)

A Closer Look at the Information Security Analyst

The information security analyst is essentially a technical role requiring proficiency in various information systems and networks. As with many technical roles, the information security analyst position has entry-, intermediate-, and senior-level roles. The entry-level roles are usually designated by the title "security analyst," the intermediate level by "security engineer," and senior level by "security architect."

These roles are responsible for configuring, delivering, administering, and monitoring security software such as firewalls, intrusion prevention and detection systems, and identity and access control management systems in line with the organization's security policies. In coordination with systems and network administrators, the security analyst diagnoses and troubleshoots security-related issues and security incidents. The person in this role must demonstrate expertise in core foundations of information technology administration, networking, protocols, and routing. Then, building on this foundation, the individual must understand the security aspects (threat, vulnerability, attack) of technology administration, delivery, and troubleshooting.

If necessary, follow the guidelines in the "Anatomy of a Technical Job Requisition" section in chapter 1 for more information, or obtain greater clarity from your organization's account manager or hiring manager about the requirements of the position. Information from those sources may help you understand when you have identified the right candidate.

Looking at the job description in figure 11.2, you will notice that the must-haves are underlined. These are the points that will be further analyzed. Review this job description, keeping the following two questions in mind: (1) Why does the hiring manager desire this skill? (2) How will this help the candidate perform better at this job?

The Information Security Engineer Job Description

The information security engineer configures, administers, monitors, and troubleshoots security software in the organization to ensure the confidentiality, integrity, and availability of information systems.

Responsibilities

  (1) <u>Day-to-day administration and maintenance</u> of security technologies

  (2) Work with IT and business units to <u>identify security requirements</u>, using risk and business impact assessments

  (3) Perform <u>security testing and vulnerability assessments</u> to identify strengths and weaknesses of organizational systems and perform remediation

  (4) Participate in <u>incident management and response activities</u>, assisting in triage, response and mitigation, and forensic analyses

  (5) Analyze and <u>evaluate current and future threat landscape</u>

Requirements

  (1) 7+ years' general information technology experience

  (2) 5+ years' experience in information security administration

  (3) Experience with at least one of these environments: UNIX/Linux, Windows, Solaris

  (4) Experience in <u>networking fundamentals</u> (TCP/IP, VLANs, DNS)

  (5) Experience in security vulnerability and penetration testing

  (6) Experience with security tools, protocols, and concepts such as firewalls, vulnerability scanning, VPN, intrusion detection and prevention

  (7) Experience with <u>information security frameworks</u> (e.g., NIST, OWASP, ISO 27001) and regulatory compliance (e.g., PCI, SOX, HIPAA)

  (8) Professional certifications (e.g., CISSP, CCSP, CISA, others)

Figure 11.4. Sample information security engineer job description

Responsibilities and Requirements Analysis

Day-to-day administration and maintenance. The main responsibilities of the information security engineer involve daily operations-based security activities—that is, to implement, deploy, and maintain security technologies and perform continuous improvements to support the organization's information security goals. As a hands-on technical specialist, the information security engineer sets up security systems such as firewalls, intrusion prevention and detection systems, encryption, and access control systems.

Security testing and vulnerability assessments. Given that the security engineer's role involves maintaining a secure environment, one of the activities this person performs to ensure that the environment is indeed secure is to test and assess the system's vulnerabilities. After all, how can one really say that their environment is secure if one does not try to break it? Hence, the goal of security testing and vulnerability assessment is to identify specific vulnerabilities and perform remediation activities to eliminate them. Penetration testing is one of the methods used in testing the information systems environment for vulnerabilities.

Incident management and response activities. When a security incident is reported, the security engineer also helps the incident management team to investigate and restore the interrupted systems to normal operations. The security engineer's skills in networking and systems administration are put into play to reduce the impact of the interruption caused by the security incident and perform root cause analysis to identify the cause of the incident. Depending on the organization's size, goals, and structure, incidence management tasks may be a stand-alone role or merged with the security engineer's role.

Evaluate current and future threat landscape. Since information security threats are dynamic and constantly changing, it is important that the security engineer keep abreast of different variations and evolutions of current and future threats and vulnerabilities by participating in industry groups and associations targeted at cybersecurity (e.g., ISACs, ISACA).

Networking fundamentals. This skill set is fundamental to any security-related role. The security engineer job role is an extension and upgrade from the core networking and systems engineer roles. Hence, one needs to have the core networking and systems engineer skill sets to perform well as a security engineer. Another reason that networking fundamentals are essential for the security engineer role is because security incidents pass through networks and thrive in the interconnectivity that exists between networked systems (LAN, WAN, internet). A security incident that occurs on a stand-alone system can damage only that one system. However, when systems are connected through networks, the impact is greater and costlier. Hence, demonstrated knowledge and experience in networking systems and protocols is key for the security engineer role (e.g., routers, VPN, TCP/IP, FTP, OSI).

Information security frameworks. Because of the importance of information security to a wide spectrum of operations, including national security, organizations' business operations, the society, and our individual lives, several organizations have created security frameworks that are used as standards and guidelines for implementing security. Some of the frameworks are mandatory (e.g., SOX, HIPAA, PCI), while others are suggested standards and guidelines (e.g., NIST, ISO, SANS). Adherence to the frameworks depends on the organization's industry alignment. For example, a health care organization must adhere to the HIPAA security and privacy framework and rules. Online retailers that collect and process payment information must adhere to the PCI framework, and financial institutions must adhere to the SOX framework. Similarly, security engineers in any of these organizations must understand and apply the security frameworks used in their industry to their information systems operations.

Questions for the Candidate

Now that you understand the role of the information security engineer, following are a few sample questions you might ask your candidate (and reasons for asking them). These will help you further understand their experience and skills to gauge their fit with your job description.

- "Would you please tell me about your network?"
  - o While there is no right or wrong answer for this question, it does provide a backdrop for subsequent questions. Please ensure that you (the recruiter) have established a rapport and that the candidate understands that you are a recruiter for company XYZ and not a social engineer who is fishing for information.
- "How does information security get done in your organization? That is, what is the goal of information security (see previous section for the goal of information security)?"
  - o The answer to this question gives you an idea of how the candidate views information security, its seriousness, its consequences, and his or her approach to being part of the solution.
- "Given the difference between threats and vulnerabilities, which would you tackle first, and what are some strategies for tackling threats/vulnerabilities?"
  - o Recalling the initial descriptions of the difference between threats and vulnerabilities, you will want to know if the candidate understands the difference. Since much of information security protection revolves around these concepts, it is key for the candidate to know the difference.
- "Since this is one of the most commonly encountered issues in web security, I'm confident you already know this. What is cross-site scripting and what is your experience defending against it?"
  - o This can be an easy or difficult question to answer. Information security professionals encounter this question in most interviews. Any security engineer needs to be able to describe what XSS is.

What We Learned

- The basics of information systems security include the protection of hardware, software, data, procedures, and people in terms of three goals: confidentiality, integrity, and availability.
- Confidentiality is the hiding of information and making it available only to authorized persons or systems that need to know the information.
- Integrity in information security refers to the quality of being unaltered, uncorrupted, and whole. Integrity is intertwined with trustworthiness.
- Availability in information security is the requirement for information to be accessible to the user when it is needed and without delays.
- A threat is the potential for an event, incident, or circumstance to have an adverse effect on an information system.
- A vulnerability is a weakness in an information system that can be attacked.
- An attack is the actual violation of security. An attack occurs when a vulnerability is successfully exploited.

CHAPTER 12

CLOUD COMPUTING

In This Chapter

- What is cloud computing?
- types of cloud computing
- pros and cons of cloud computing
- cloud computing technologies
- study of a cloud computing job description
- review of a cloud computing candidate

What Is Cloud Computing?

Cloud computing is convenient, on-demand network access to a shared pool of configurable computing resources (e.g., networks, servers, storage, applications, and services) that can be quickly deployed with little management overhead (Mell & Grance 2011). In other words, it represents a computing style where scalable computing resources are provided to users as a *service* through the internet. Cloud computing services are provided on a pay-as-you-go model. This means that consumers pay only for what they need, when they need it. In recent years, cloud computing represents an important and evolving information technology paradigm shift.

There are three main cloud services available and three ways that cloud services can be delivered to users.

Cloud Services Models

- *Software as a Service (SaaS)*: This is a category of cloud services whereby a cloud provider makes its applications or software available to the consumer to access from their computers, mobile devices, browsers, and so on. The idea here is that the cloud provider manages and controls the cloud application (network, servers, operating system, storage, etc.). The cloud services provider provides all software, hardware, and operating systems so that the user does not need to worry about how the service is supported or how the underlying infrastructure is managed. The user or organization purchases/subscribes to the service, and the service is ready in a short amount of time. Examples of SaaS are Microsoft Office 365, Salesforce.com, and Google Apps.
- *Platform as a Service (PaaS)*: This is a cloud service whereby the cloud provider makes its platform available to the consumer. It allows consumers to install, develop, and manage their own applications (on the available platform) without the headache of purchasing and maintaining their own hardware infrastructure. This service model is used primarily by developers. It allows them to design, build, and test their applications and then deliver those applications to end users from the cloud provider's resources. An example could be a lone software developer who has a great idea about the next "killer app." Rather than invest in purchasing, installing, and configuring the right hardware, software, OS, and so on, the developer needs only to pay a subscription fee to a cloud services provider to use these resources.
- *Infrastructure as a Service (IaaS)*: This is a type of cloud service whereby the cloud vendor provides a virtualized environment to the consumer through the internet. This typically includes servers, storage, network, security, and sometimes even a physical

datacenter environment, also known as a *complete infrastructure.* The cloud vendor provides the infrastructure, and the consumer installs, configures, and manages the installation of operating and other desired software at a pay-as-you-go fee. AWS and Microsoft Azure are examples of IaaS.

Table 12.1 below depicts the different cloud services and their primary users.

Cloud Service	Primary User	Description	Type of Infrastructure
SaaS	Consumers and end users	Cloud provider hosts end-user software in the cloud that users can access using the internet.	Hosted applications

PaaS	Developers	Cloud provider hosts development environment in the cloud, allowing programmers to develop, test, and deliver their own software to consumers.	Developer tools, database systems, operating system
IaaS	IT organizations	Cloud provider hosts the whole IT infrastructure on the cloud. (Think of any infrastructure that allows an organization function.)	Servers, storage, networking, firewall, security, operating system

Table 12.1. Cloud services and their primary users

Cloud Delivery Models

- *Private cloud*: This is when the cloud service infrastructure is created and provided by a single organization to suit its needs and made available to its employees. This cloud service and its infrastructure is owned, configured, and operated by the organization for the organization's exclusive use. In this type of delivery, the cloud infrastructure may be hosted on-premises or in a co-location data center. The main concerns are the cost and time to set up and maintain the cloud infrastructure.

- *Public cloud*: This is when the cloud service infrastructure is provisioned for public use. In this case, a third-party cloud provider operates a shared-cloud service environment that is accessible to potential users. Concerns for this type of cloud delivery model are security, privacy, control, and data ownership.

- *Hybrid cloud*: This is a mixture of private and public models. It is when an organization works with one or many third-party cloud providers to create a cloud infrastructure. It's the best of both worlds. In this model, the organization integrates its private cloud infrastructure with those of one or two public cloud services providers. This model does a few things: it keeps some of the organization's infrastructure private; it extends the capacity of the private cloud to a public cloud; and it gains capacity, saving time and cost of maintenance.

Table 12.2 below depicts different cloud services and their providers.

Cloud Providers	Cloud Service	Examples
AWS	PaaS IaaS	Amazon Elastic Compute Cloud (Amazon EC2) Amazon Simple Storage Service (Amazon S3)
Microsoft	SaaS PaaS IaaS	Microsoft Office 365 Microsoft Azure Microsoft Azure
Google	SaaS PaaS IaaS	Google Apps, G Suite Google Cloud Platform (Google App Engine) Google App Engine
Salesforce.com	SaaS	Software for sales, marketing, customer service
Oracle	SaaS PaaS IaaS	Oracle Cloud Applications (HR, ERP, CRM) Oracle Platform Oracle Infrastructure

Table 12.2. Cloud services and providers

Why Organizations Migrate to the Cloud

Organizations are always looking to make decisions that save cost and time, allow growth, and, mostly, affect the bottom line positively. Such decisions are made in all business operations but especially in information technology services. From what we have learned about cloud services from the previous sections, we can see that they offer several benefits to organizations in terms of cost and time as well as allowing organizations to grow their operations. Cloud services provide flexibility and scalable IT.

This means organizations have the flexibility to request changes in their IT services and can increase or reduce their use with minimal financial investment. This is what Amazon.com and NIST refer to as "elastic," meaning cloud-based computing resources can be increased or decreased automatically and rapidly, depending on demand. See table 12.3 below for cases and scenarios in which organizations engage cloud services.

Purpose	Scenario
New product awareness	Suppose an organization is planning to run a one-week TV ad for a new product. This ad is expected to drive millions of people to their website. The organization knows their website is incapable of accepting a million views without crashing, so they engage their cloud vendor to expand the bandwidth resources on their website for a month until the effect of the ad wears off and page views taper off. In this case, the organization pays for only one month of additional resources.
New application development	Suppose a software company is starting a product and needs twenty new developers to work on the application. Instead of purchasing twenty high-powered computers, twenty database server licenses, application development frameworks, and so on, and setting them up, they can engage a PaaS cloud vendor to provide the platform and development resources already installed and configured. The developers can immediately start doing their jobs. This makes it easy to increase or decrease developers as the project continues.

Table 12.3. Cloud services scenarios

A report from Gartner (2017) shows that health care organizations spend nearly 75 percent of their IT budget on maintenance of the internal information systems. Hence, one might venture to say that infrastructure implementation costs (hardware, software, personnel), capital expenses, operating expenses, indirect cost, infrastructure maintenance, ensuring availability of services, security, and performance provide the motivation for moving to the cloud.

Pros and Cons of Cloud

Even though there are many benefits to migrating to the cloud, cloud services are not without some risks. Concerns for security, privacy, data ownership, and loss of control are some of the risk factors that plague cloud services. In fact, a recent survey found that concerns about cloud security remain very high. When asked about their biggest concerns regarding cloud security, the survey participants indicated data loss (57 percent), data privacy (49 percent), and confidentiality (47 percent) (PRNewswire 2017).

Since many organizations are migrating to the cloud, it makes cloud vendors a potential target for cybercriminals. For example, Microsoft's cloud withstands about 1.5 million hacking attempts daily (Microsoft 2017). It is no wonder organizations are concerned that hackers may break into their cloud vendor's services and access their data. Indeed, there have been several occurrences of security breaches of cloud vendors. This is why cloud service providers are gearing up with best-in-class security features, so much so that even the CIA purchases cloud services from Amazon AWS (*The Atlantic* 2014). Furthermore, Microsoft has over 3,500 security engineers that help keep its cloud systems secure (Microsoft 2017).

Organizations are also concerned about losing control of the management of their data. As you can imagine, the benefits of using cloud services may sometimes outweigh this risk. In addition, cloud service providers are known to have options for allaying such concerns. If the CIA, NASA, and the FDA chose to use Amazon AWS and Microsoft Azure (*The Atlantic* 2014), it speaks volumes about the ability of these cloud providers to mitigate this concern and others, such as privacy and data ownership. Table 12.4 shows a summary of the pros and cons of cloud services for cloud use versus on premise.

Factors	No Cloud (on premise)	Cloud
Cost	Initial cost, operating cost, personnel expertise can be prohibitive	Pay-as-you-go for only what is needed; minimal capital investment.
Elastic Resources	Lack of flexibility for growth	Flexibility and scalability for growth; ideal for unplanned business events
Control	Organizations gain control over their data	Organizations lose control over their data
Security and Privacy	Organizations can manage security and privacy of their data	Organizations lose control over the management of security and privacy of their data

Table 12.4. Summary of pros and cons of cloud and on-premise infrastructure

Cloud Computing Technologies and Processes

This section lists the main cloud technologies and processes that recruiters will encounter in job descriptions and résumés. These technologies and processes make up the skill sets that candidates need for a successful job interview and career in this field.

Public Cloud

As described previously, public cloud refers to cloud services delivered by cloud providers that operate shared-cloud environments and make them accessible and available to the public. The major public cloud providers are Amazon AWS, Microsoft Azure, and Google Cloud Platform. Cloud professionals should be very familiar with the inner workings of at least one of these cloud services providers. Below is an example of public cloud skill set requirements for a cloud engineer.

Sample Job Requirements
- Experience architecting solutions within AWS and Microsoft Azure
- Experience with the AWS Product Suite (EC2, S3, RDS, CloudFormation, Redshift, Lambda, EMR)
- Knowledge of these public cloud service providers: AWS and Microsoft Azure

Web Services, API, and REST

Web services allow different computer systems on the internet to talk to one another (interoperability). Application programming interfaces (APIs) allow communications also but use an interface to facilitate communication between different applications. Web API is a web service with an API. An application can communicate with another application using an API, but when the communication is facilitated over a network, a web service is required.

In a web services world, Representational State Transfer (REST) defines every web service as a resource. A resource is a generic term for a file, document, or anything that can be addressed or identified on the web. Using REST allows these resources to be lightweight and stateless (i.e., sender and receiver information are not retained). These are desirable elements for cloud computing environments that underlie the cloud architecture.

A cloud professional should have demonstrable experience with these patterns of service on the internet and know the protocols and technologies that make this possible. Below is an example of web services, API, and REST skill set requirements for a cloud engineer.

Sample Job Requirements
- Experience with web (REST) APIs, Nova API
- Experience with web services and APIs and with RESTful and SOAP

Cloud Security

As described previously, security is a concern for cloud services subscribers. DeltaRisk, a cybersecurity company, notes that even though cloud services like AWS, Azure, and Google provide cost savings and flexibility, the cloud systems administrators and developers who implement these migrations sometimes lack the adequate security knowledge required to secure data (PRNewswire 2017).

It is no wonder that anyone interested in working as a cloud administrator is expected to not only know their way around cloud security but also to understand why it is important. The demand for candidates who understand those reasons is why some job descriptions in this area require security and risk-management certifications. Below is an example of cloud security skill set requirements for a cloud engineer.

Sample Job Requirements
- Experience with network security, wireless security, application security
- Experience with infrastructure hardening and security baselines, web server and database security
- Experience working with intrusion detection, antivirus, log analysis, network security, patching
- CISSP certification, CISM/CISA, or CRISC a plus

Database Technologies

Traditional database systems such as MySQL, Microsoft SQL Server, or PostgreSQL are common in the cloud. PaaS routinely provision databases as part of the products offered in this delivery model. Hence, a cloud engineer should be familiar with the common ones. The cloud engineer does not need to be an expert programmer but does need to know how to configure databases. Database administration skills are called for here. Below is an example of database skill set requirements for a cloud engineer.

Sample Job Requirements
- Strong experience with NoSQL and SQL
- Experience in database configuration, performance tuning, troubleshooting, backups, high availability
- Familiarity with database technologies such as MySQL, MS SQL, RDS, Azure Cosmos DB, or PostgreSQL

DevOps and Systems Automation

DevOps is a term that describes the combination of practices and tools in "development" and "operations"—that is, software development and IT operations. The idea behind this compound term is to remove the boundaries separating the software development and operations departments, which were traditionally two departments with different philosophies. Removing the boundaries that separated these teams meant they could collaborate, communicate, and share goals about efficiency and effectiveness with the goal of improving IT service delivery.

You guessed it! The emphasis on DevOps represents the need to deliver IT services and applications (IT delivery) to customers at a rapid pace. Coincidentally, rapid IT service delivery is one of the building blocks of cloud services. Hence, the DevOps skill set fits very well as a requirement for cloud engineers.

Please note that although DevOps is usually a job title in itself, cloud engineers are expected to apply DevOps practices as part of their jobs. The processes and tools used for DevOps are somewhat different from those used in traditional software development. DevOps practices include *continuous integration, continuous delivery,* and *infrastructure as code* as well as configuration management and automation. The DevOps is all about speed, delivery, and reliability. (The three new italicized practices introduced above are defined below.)

- *Continuous Integration*: integrate or merge code changes in version control, ready for build and test
- *Continuous Delivery*: automatically build and test code changes, ready for production release
- *Infrastructure as Code*: programmatically configure infrastructure rather than doing so manually

The cloud engineer needs a good understanding of these practices—or at the very least a DevOps mind-set. Below is an example of DevOps and system automation skill set requirements for a cloud engineer.

Sample Job Requirements
- DevOps mindset with a continuous delivery mind-set and expertise with cloud technologies
- Experience with Infrastructure as Code tools (e.g., Chef, Cloudformation, Puppet, and Ansible)
- Experience writing code to automate processes using Python, Ruby, and Perl
- Experience automating build processes for functionality and scale testing
- Experience developing automation processes and tools to make deploying and supporting simpler and faster

Programming Languages

From the previous description of the DevOps system and automation skill sets, it is obvious that cloud engineers need a good understanding of scripting languages such as Python, Perl, and Ruby. The level of programming experience required for a cloud engineer is a lot less than is required for a software developer. However, the cloud engineer does need to have this experience since it is necessary for scripting automation solutions. Below is an example of scripting and programming language skill set requirements for a cloud engineer.

Sample Job Requirements
- Familiarity with Python
- Fluency in the associated programming languages (e.g., Ruby, Python, PowerShell, or any other scripting language)

Operating System and Networking

As of January 2018, Amazon AWS has the largest market share for public cloud services, followed closely by Microsoft Azure (CNBC 2018). Amazon AWS uses Ubuntu Linux as its primary operating system. This suggests that Ubuntu Linux is the most used operating system for cloud services, followed by Microsoft Azure. Cloud engineers need experience in UNIX/Linux and Windows OS. It is also expected that cloud engineers be experienced at network administration and configuration using these OSs.

Sample Job Requirements
- Network expertise—Linux kernel network features, routing
- Strong experience with Linux environments
- Familiar with UNIX and Windows servers and their networking requirements
- Working knowledge of Ethernet, TCP/IP, and routing protocols
- Experience with Windows and Linux operating systems

The Cloud Engineer Job Description

If necessary, follow the guidelines in the "Anatomy of a Technical Job Requisition" section in chapter 1 for more information or obtain greater clarity from your organization's account manager or hiring manager about the requirements of the position. Information from those sources can help technical recruiters recognize when they have identified the right candidate.

Looking at the job description in figure 12.1, you will notice that the must-haves are underlined. These are the points that will be further analyzed. Review this job description with the following two questions in mind: (1) Why does the hiring manager desire this skill? (2) How will this help the candidate perform better at this job?

The cloud engineer leverages public cloud resources to build, develop, and administer a cloud environment. He or she has experience in Amazon AWS and Microsoft Azure public clouds and uses DevOps processes to deliver services to clients.

Responsibilities
  (1) Design, build, and operate cloud services and capabilities using AWS and Azure
  (2) Identify security issues and risks and develop mitigation plans
  (3) Perform regular scripting work as needed (shell scripting, Python, JavaScript, etc.)
  (4) Adopt a DevOps role, identifying issues and writing infrastructure as code to automate the resolution of the problem

Requirements
  (1) 5+ years of network engineering experience
  (2) 4+ years of experience with public cloud: Amazon AWS, Microsoft Azure
  (3) 2+ years of experience with software development and scripting (Python, Ruby, JavaScript)
  (4) Experience with DevOps practices and automation of software testing, delivery, and infrastructure changes (continuous integration, infrastructure as code)
  (5) Expertise in Windows and Linux system administration
  (6) Experience in databases (Relational and NoSQL)

Figure 12.2. Sample job description—cloud engineer

Responsibilities and Requirements Analysis

The underlined skill sets and requirements have been discussed previously. However, each skill set was discussed as an independent skill set. In this job description, the skill sets and requirements are combined and paint a clearer picture of what the cloud engineer does and the skill set required for the job role.

AWS and Azure. The main responsibility of the cloud engineer is to build and deliver services through cloud. For this job, the engineer is building and delivering services using Amazon AWS and Microsoft Azure, which are the most widely used public cloud service providers.

Security issues and risks. Security remains a major issue in cloud services for the cloud providers and their customers. Whether it is explicitly stated in a cloud engineer's job description or not, it is expected that the cloud engineer understand security in the cloud.

Infrastructure as code (IAC). IAC refers to the ability to write code that automates the provisioning of infrastructure services. This is a task that comes with the DevOps process. Traditionally, engineers would manually configure options on applications. With IAC, the engineer needs only to code and run an IAC script that automates the configuration needed.

Network engineering experience. The underlying or prerequisite experience for a cloud engineer is network engineering. As the foundation upon which cloud services stand, it is expected and required that a cloud engineer have prior networking experience. The role of a cloud engineer (like the architect role) is one in which *prior experience with another role* usually provides the necessary preparation, rather than educational/training knowledge.

Review of a Cloud Engineer Candidate

Now that you understand the role of the cloud engineer, following are a few sample questions you might ask your candidate (and reasons for asking them). The questions will help you further understand their experience and skills to gauge their fit with your job description.

- "Would you please tell me about your experience as a cloud engineer?"
    o This is mostly a question/request that relaxes candidates (and perhaps the recruiter), giving them the space to tell you a little or a lot about their experience as a cloud engineer. Since their answer provides a backdrop for subsequent questions, please listen to hear key terms you have learned from this chapter. You can use those to form follow-up questions, if necessary.
- "Although this position is for a cloud engineer and not necessarily a DevOps person, there are a fair number of DevOps roles played by the cloud engineer. Please tell me about any specific experience you have using DevOps processes in your position as a cloud engineer."
    o DevOps is very intertwined with cloud positions, and you want to understand the candidate's exposure or experience with DevOps processes: continuous integration, continuous delivery, infrastructure as code, collaboration, automation, and configurations.
- "My understanding of infrastructure as code is that it is a very good skill to have as a cloud engineer, especially when working with the AWS product suite. Please tell me about your experience using IAC to manage infrastructure at a code level."
    o With the evolution of cloud services, IAC is high-level skill set that lets you know the candidate's expertise level. Remember that knowing about IAC is distinct from production experience of managing infrastructure at a code level, so you are listening for real-life experiences and scenarios in which code was used for adding or configuring storage, memory, CPU, and so on.
- "With cloud services requiring 24/7 availability, what's your experience in monitoring performance and logs to identify opportunities for updates or even potential issues?"

    o   Cloud availability and reliability are very important to cloud vendors and their customers. Picture a downtime at a major airline because of cloud issues! This question helps you understand the candidate and the level of importance he or she ascribes to availability, performance, and solving availability problems. Ideally, you are listening to hear some level of accountability and ownership of availability problems. You are also listening to hear about the tools they used to monitor systems at each architectural tier (application, server, database).

What We Learned

- Cloud computing is convenient, on-demand network access to a shared and elastic pool of computing resources that can be quickly deployed with little management effort.
- There are three main cloud services available and three ways that cloud services can be delivered to users.
- Cloud services models are Software as a Service (SaaS), Platform as a Service (PaaS), and Infrastructure as a Service (IaaS).
- Cloud delivery models are private cloud, public cloud, and hybrid cloud.
- Concerns about security, privacy, data ownership, and loss of control are some of the risk factors that plague the adoption of cloud services.
- DevOps is a term that describes the combination of practices and tools in "development" and "operations"—that is, software development and IT operations.
- DevOps practices include continuous integration, continuous delivery, infrastructure as code, configuration management, and automation.

CHAPTER 13

CERTIFICATIONS

In This Chapter

- the value of certification
- the question of certification
- security certifications
- software development certifications
- database certifications
- operating systems and cloud certifications
- networking certifications

A certification is a credential earned to indicate one's knowledge and skills. Certifications are used for evaluating an individual's ability to apply knowledge in practice. Acquiring certification in any field indicates a professional level of competence in the principles and practices associated with that profession.

A certification does not guarantee that a candidate is an expert in a field but rather shows that the candidate has the potential to be effective in a specific field. It also demonstrates the candidate's ability to learn and strive for new career heights.

In this chapter, we review the certification requirements of organizations, answering the question "Why do organizations need a certified candidate?" This chapter also reveals the certification requirements for operating systems and networking, programming, information security, cloud, database, business analysis, and project management.

The Value of Certification

Though one school of thought claims that certification was created by software vendors to popularize their products, software vendors argue that certification increases the value and the earning power of the candidate. This may have been true a decade ago when the craze was on for certifications such as MCSE (Microsoft Certified Systems Engineer) and CCNA (Cisco Certified Network Associate). At that time, hiring companies wanted to prove they had the best-skilled people working for them, and the candidates wanted the prestige accorded to a certified individual.

Nowadays, it is unclear who gets the most value from certifications. Is it the vendor, whose name appears as a prefix on the titles of hundreds of thousands of individuals, thereby creating an increased awareness for the vendor's products? Or is it the candidate, who is looking for a boost in their career and thinks that certification will do just that? Does it really matter? Both parties seem to be gaining something; it's a win-win for all, even though one party (the bigger guy) may be getting more out of it than the other.

The value of IT certification has been watered down during the years following its crazed beginnings in the 1990s. When the craze began, it was assumed that individuals were required to go through classroom training programs to take the associated test. The training classes added real value to the program because individuals sat together in a classroom and learned how to install, configure, and troubleshoot applications.

This was the case for a long time until self-study books hit the shelves and people opted to study and take the test without attending an expensive training class. The result has been an increased number of certified candidates. One may argue that the effect of the proliferation of certified individuals in the industry is the diminished value of certifications. However, this is not nearly the case.

In 2018, the value of technical certifications is still high among IT professionals. Indeed, information security was ranked number one by IT professionals and IT leaders as the certification that provided the most value, in a study by TekSystems (2018). Further, in a PearsonVue (2016) survey of 28,000 individuals in top-ranked technology organizations, 65 percent of the participants noted that certifications had a positive impact on their career; about 26 percent said it helped advance their careers; 20 percent received a salary increase; and 19 percent found a job. Clearly, value is still perceived in technical certifications.

Although cheating on certification exams is a concern, software organizations such as Microsoft, Oracle, and Cisco, which provide the certification exams, are making changes to minimize the impact of cheating. For example, test makers are changing the exam format, adding practical elements and increasing the penalty for cheating.

Experience over Certification

At first glance, experience may seem superior to certification. However, certification is a clearer and faster means of determining skill sets on paper or in an online résumé.

There are reasons why hiring managers prefer candidates with certifications. A good question to ask your hiring manager is this: "If presented with two candidates, one certified and the other not, which would you choose if both seem to have the required experience?" The hiring manager's response may depend on the following three factors. The first is prior certification—that is, whether the hiring manager has been certified at one time or other. Second, the hiring manager's perceived value of certifications may inform his or her preference. Third is the level of expertise needed for the job (high versus low). For more technical positions such as information security, systems administration, and ethical hacking, certification may be a factor in favor of hiring a person. However, if the position requires soft skills, business skills, and technical skills (like those usually found in business analysts), certification may be of less value to the hiring manager. This is because the skill sets for business analysts are more business related and thus can sometimes be acquired through experience rather than via tests and certifications.

The Question of Certification

"Why certification?" really contains two questions: (1) Why does a candidate need to be certified, and (2) why does an employer need a certified individual?

In answer to the first question, one of the reasons candidates get certified in the IT industry is to call more attention to themselves and their skills to let potential employers know that they possess the required competency in the skill in question. According to the PearsonVue (2016) survey, some of the reasons individuals obtain certification are (1) employer requirement, (2) subject matter knowledge acquisition, (3) to improve professional profile, and (4) requirement from profession. There are some professions for which certifications are almost always a requirement. The requirement may not be explicit, but it is still an unwritten requirement. Examples of professions with this underlying requirement are networking and information security. If you do a cursory survey of open postings in these two professions, you will find certification among the job requirements for most of them.

Do candidates need certification to prove their ability to perform? The answers are *yes*, *no*, and *it depends*.

> Do candidates need certification to prove their ability to perform?

The answer is *yes* for candidates who have something to prove (usually candidates with one to three years of experience in the desired field), *yes* for candidates who can take the time to improve on their skills, *yes* for candidates who are looking for advancement, *yes* for those who want the chance to prove they can perform as well as the next person, and *yes* for those who have an aptitude for learning and growing.

On the other hand, there are some very skilled workers who do not need a piece of paper or badge to prove they can deliver on the job. They are usually candidates who have several years of experience in their specified field and have neither the time nor the patience for certifications.

Why does an employer need a certified individual? As a technical recruiter with a certification requirement listed in a job requisition, you must seek to understand the reasoning behind this requirement. Here are some of the reasons employers may require certification:

o   The employer is in an industry that requires certified employees to maintain their license to practice.
o   The employer may have identified certification as a good trait in current employees and wants to ensure that future employees have that proven trait as well.
o   The employer might be a vendor partner and, as such, may have a vendor partnership requirement to employ several certified individuals.

These are just a few reasons. It's your job to find out exactly why the hiring manager requires a certified individual when a noncertified but experienced person could suffice.

Certified versus Noncertified Profile

There are many qualified candidates available with the experience needed but without the certification. These same candidates will rarely seek certifications unless they are out of work or between jobs.

Figure 13.1. Profile of a noncertified candidate (NCC)

The profile of a noncertified candidate, as illustrated in figure 13.1, shows that this person (1) has worked for the same company for more than five years and is not looking to change organizations; (2) has more than ten years of experience in a particular field; (3) scorns the certification process; (4) immediately dislikes organizations that require certification over experience; and (5) when faced with interviewing a certified candidate, will be the toughest interviewer to please. As an interviewer, this noncertified, experienced person wants to ensure that the candidate has more knowledge than what is presented on the résumé.

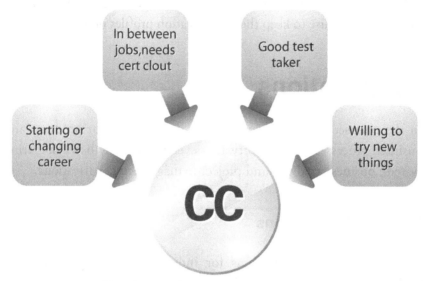

Figure 13.2. Profile of a certified candidate (CC)

A look at figure 13.2 illustrates that the certified candidate may be (1) starting or changing careers; (2) in between jobs and needing the added clout of a certification; (3) a good test taker; or (4) more willing to try new things.

Certification Profile Verification

A recent report found that employers rarely verify their candidate's certifications (TekSystems 2018)—that is, whether the certification is valid, up to date, or expired. If certifications are important for the hiring decision, it might be important to verify the status. It is especially important in the technology field, where changes are rapid.

These technological changes also change the certifications. Windows Server configuration in 2005 is no longer the same today. Individuals may have been certified at one time for a software application, and because they did not recertify or renew their certification, it expired. Some professionals update their résumé to indicate that their certification has expired; for example, you may see *MCSE 2017 (expired)*. Others do not update their résumé to indicate the state of their certifications if expired, perhaps for lack of time or for other reasons. Today, there are "badging" applications that individuals use to keep their certification profiles up to date.

Certifications

In the next section, we review certifications for vendor products and business processes such as software development, database, operating system, business analysis, and project management certifications.

Security Certifications

There are many certifications for individuals seeking to validate their information security skills. Certifications are available from several organizations such as the International Information Systems Security Certification Consortium (ISC²), Information Systems Audit and Control Association (ISACA), SANS, and Global Information Assurance Certification (GAIC). Table 13.1 below presents most common certifications and the skills they validate.

Organization	Acronym	Certification	Validates:
ISC²	CISSP	Certified Information Systems Security Professional	Knowledge and ability to manage overall security
	SSCP	Systems Security Certified Practitioner	Ability to administer IT infrastructure using security policies
	CCSP	Certified Cloud Security Professional	Knowledge to administer cloud security architecture

ISACA	CISA	Certified Information Systems Auditor	Skills in audit, control, security, assurance, and compliance
	CISM	Certified Information Security Manager	Skills in managing enterprise information security programs
	CRISC	Certified in Risk and Information Systems Control	Skills in IT risk management and enterprise risk management
GIAC	GISF	GIAC Information Security Fundamentals	Skills in network protection and host protection
	GSEC	GIAC Security Essentials	Skills in attack prevention and intrusion detection
	GPEN	GIAC Certified Penetration Tester	Skills in penetration testing and ethical hacking

Table 13.1. Security certifications and skills validated

Software Development Certifications

We review software development certifications such as those for development platforms from Microsoft and Java. Software development certifications from Microsoft and Java have evolved through the years and will continue to do so, as long as technologies change. Table 13.2 below lists the more common development certifications from Microsoft and Oracle as well as the skills that the certifications validate.

Organization	Acronym	Certification	Validates:
Microsoft	MCSD	Microsoft Certified Solution Developer: App Builder	Skills to design and build web and mobile applications and services
	MCSA	Microsoft Certified Solution Associate: Web Applications	Expertise at implementing modern web applications
Oracle	OCE	Oracle Certified Expert: JPA	Skills to build Java Persistence API for back-end functionality
	OCE	Oracle Certified Expert: Developer	Skills to build applications using Java Enterprise JavaBeans Developer

Table 13.2. Software development certifications and skills validated

Database Certifications

In this section, we review the certifications from Microsoft and Oracle for database administration, development, business intelligence, and big data tracks. Oracle certification *requires* that candidates attend classroom training before they can be certified on most of their technologies. This requirement can be expensive for the individual but almost always guarantees the individual has proven knowledge of the product. In both organizations' certifications, the *associate* notation indicates that certifications are entry level and prerequisites to the *expert* or *professional* certification. Table 13.3 below lists the more common database certifications.

Organization	Acronym	Certification	Validates:
Microsoft	MCSA	Microsoft Certified Solution Associate: Database Administration	Skills with database installation, maintenance, configuration, and provisioning
	MCSA	Microsoft Certified Solution Associate: Database Development	Skills in development and analytics for on-premise and cloud-based databases
	MCSA	Microsoft Certified Solution Associate: Business Intelligence	Skills in ETL, data warehouse, and OLAP
	MCSA	Microsoft Certified Solution Associate: Data Engineering with Azure	Demonstrates expertise in data engineering and cloud services
	MCSA	Microsoft Certified Solution Associate: Machine Learning	Demonstrates expertise in working with Microsoft Azure, machine learning, big data, and SQL R
	MCSE	Microsoft Certified Solutions Expert: Data Management and Analytics	Skills in building solutions across multiple technologies both on premise and in the cloud

Oracle		Oracle Advanced PL/SQL Developer Certified Professional	Skills in database development using SQL and PL/SQL
		Oracle Database Administrator Certified Associate	Skills in database administration using Oracle 11g/12c or newest database version
		Oracle Database Performance Tuning Certified Expert	Skill in database administration and performance tuning

Table 13.3. Database certifications and skills validated

Project Management Certifications

The Project Management Institute (PMI) offers several certifications that test the ability of candidates to manage projects and apply standards during project delivery. Like the business analysis certification, the requirements for project management certification are not as easy as what is found in technical certification. The more popular project management certifications are the Project Management Professional (PMP) and Program Management Professional (PgMP).

o *Project Management Professional (PMP)*: From the PMI certification information, the PMP certification demonstrates knowledge and skill in leading and directing project teams and in delivering project results within the constraints of schedule, budget, and resources. Prerequisites require that only those who lead and direct teams to deliver projects within the constraints of schedule, budget, and scope are to apply to take the test; in addition, applicants are required to have a bachelor's degree, three to five years of project management experience, and thirty-five hours of project management education.

o *Program Management Professional (PgMP)*: The PMI certification information also notes that PgMP certification recognizes experience and skill in overseeing multiple related projects that are aligned within an organizational strategy. Only those who manage program activities that span functions, organizations, geographic regions, and cultures can apply. Requirements vary for bachelor's degree and high school diploma holders but include four years of project management experience and four to seven years of program management experience.

Operating Systems and Cloud Certifications

Organizations such as Microsoft, Oracle, Red Hat, and Amazon have certifications for operating systems, cloud, and DevOps. The notations *professional* and *associate* indicate expert and entry- or base-level proficiency, respectively. Cloud platform certifications generally validate skill sets for cloud-based solutions. Organizations like Red Hat are specific regarding the cloud delivery model certification: private or hybrid. Table 13.4 below lists the certifications and the skills they validate.

Organization	Acronym	Certification	Validates:
Microsoft	MCSA	Microsoft Certified Solution Associate: Cloud Platform	Skills in general cloud-related technologies emphasizing IT cost reduction
	MCSA	Microsoft Certified Solution Associate: Linux on Azure	Skills used for designing, architecting, and maintaining a Linux-based cloud using Microsoft Azure

	MCSA	Microsoft Certified Solution Associate: Windows Server	Skills using Microsoft Windows Server to deliver IT and reduce cost
	MCSE	Microsoft Certified Solutions Expert: Cloud Platform and Infrastructure	Skills in data center management, cloud technologies, identity management, systems management, virtualization, storage, and networking
Oracle	OCP	Oracle Certified Professional, Oracle Linux System Administrator	Skills in implementing and administering Oracle Linux
	OCP	Oracle Certified Professional, Oracle Solaris System Administrator	Skills in UNIX operating system, commands, and utilities, configuring network interfaces
	OCP	Oracle Cloud Infrastructure Certified Architect Associate	Skills in Oracle cloud infrastructure and general cloud computing concepts
Red Hat	RHCSA	Red Hat® Certified System Administrator: Red Hat OpenStack	Skills to create, configure, and operate private clouds using Red Hat OpenStack
	RHCS	Red Hat Certified Specialist: Hybrid Cloud Management	Skills to create, configure, and operate hybrid cloud using Red Hat CloudForms

Amazon	AWS	AWS Certified Solutions Architect: Professional	Skills in architecting and deploying secure and reliable applications using AWS technologies
	AWS	AWS Certified Developer: Associate	Skills in developing and maintaining applications on AWS
	AWS	AWS Certified DevOps Engineer: Professional	Skills in provisioning, operating, and managing distributed applications on AWS

Table 13.4. Operating system and cloud certifications and skills validated

Networking Certifications

The major networking certification organizations are Cisco and CompTIA. Cisco has certifications for different aspects of networking, including data center, wireless, collaboration, and so on. In addition, Cisco's certifications have three levels: associate, professional, and expert, with associate as the foundation level and expert as the highest expertise. CompTIA has one certification that is specific to networking. Table 13.5 below shows the certifications and the skills they validate.

Organization	Acronym	Certification	Validates:
Cisco	CCNP	Cisco Certified Network Professional: Routing and Switching	Skills in network routing and switching

	CCNP	Cisco Certified Network Professional: Data Center	Skills in designing, building, and operating a data center infrastructure
	CCNA	Cisco Certified Network Associate: Wireless	Skills in monitoring, troubleshooting, and supporting Cisco wireless networks
CompTIA	NA	CompTIA Network+	Skills in troubleshooting, configuring, and managing wired and wireless networks

Table 13.5. Networking certifications and skills validated

What We Learned

- Certification is a means to define the common body of knowledge for a particular practice and thereby evaluate an individual's ability to apply that knowledge in practice.
- Certification may have been created by vendors as a means to garner more awareness for their products, but it is also an avenue for candidates to increase their earning power.
- The value of certifications still remains high among IT professionals and IT leaders.
- The noncertified candidate has typically worked for the same company for more than five years, is not looking to change organizations, and has more than ten years of experience in a particular field, while the certified candidate may be starting or changing careers or be between jobs and in need of the added clout of certification.

BIBLIOGRAPHY

American Software Testing Qualifications Board. n.d. *Software Testing Certification*. Retrieved September 30, 2009, from ASTQB website: http://www.astqb.org/.

Beginners Co. n.d. *Visual Basic 6 Application Development Part 2*. Retrieved July 10, 2009, from Beginners.co.uk website: http://tutorials.beginners.co.uk/visual-basic-6-application-development-part-2-distributed-applications.htm#.

Booch, G., R. A. Maksimchuk, M. W. Engle, B. J. Young, J. Conallen, and K. A. Houston. 2007. *Object-Oriented Analysis and Design with Applications*. Upper Saddle River, NJ. Pearson Education, Inc.

Brooks, F. 1987. *Software Requirements*. No Silver Bullet: Essence and Accidents of Software Engineering. IEEE Computer Society Press, 10–19.

Cockerell, P. 1987. *ARM Assembly Language Programming: 1987*. Retrieved January 21, 2009, from http://www.peter-cockerell.net/aalp/.

Computer Technology Documentation Project. n.d. *Repeaters, Bridges, Routers, and Gateways*. Retrieved November 24, 2008, from the Computer Technology Documentation Project website: http://www.comptechdoc.org/independent/networking/guide/netdevices.html.

Discovery Communications. n.d. *How Stuff Works-Operating Systems*. Retrieved August 10, 2008, from How Stuff Works website: computer.howstuffworks.com.

Habraken, J., and M. Hayden. 2004. *Teach Yourself Networking in 24 Hours*. Indianapolis, IN: Sams Publishing.

Hoffer, J., George, J., and Valacichi, J. 2002. *Modern Systems Analysis and Design,* Fifth Edition. Upper Saddle River, NJ: Prentice Hall.

IBM Corporation. n.d. *IBM Academic Initiative: An Introduction to the Mainframe: Large Scale Commercial Computing.* Retrieved September 20, 2009, from IBM corporate website: http://www-03.ibm.com/systems/z/advantages/charter/skills_coursematerials.html#LargeScaleCC.

Information Management and SourceMedia, Inc. n.d. *Glossary.* Retrieved November 29, 2008, from Information Management website: www.dmreview.com/glossary/d.html.

Johnston, A. n.d. *The Role of the Agile Architect.* Retrieved September 4, 2009, from http://www.agilearchitect.org/agile/role.htm.

Kendall, K., and J. Kendall. *Systems Analysis and Design.* Englewood, NJ: Prentice Hall.

Kettner, John, Mike Ebbers, Wayne O'Brien, and Bill Ogden. August 2009. *Introduction to the New Mainframe: z/OS Basics.* Retrieved September 5, 2009, from Oracle Corporate website: www.redbooks.ibm.com/abstracts/sg246366.html?Open. IBM RedBooks.

Knowledge Rush. n.d. *Acorn RISC Machine.* Retrieved December 12, 2008, from Knowledge Rush website: http://www.knowledgerush.com/kr/encyclopedia/Acorn_RISC_Machine/.

Markiewicz, M. E., and C. J. Lucena. 2001. *Object Oriented Framework Development* Retrieved June 15, 2009, from Association of Computer Machinery website: http://www.acm.org/crossroads/xrds7-4/frameworks.html.

Microsoft Corporation. n.d. *Microsoft Learning: Microsoft Certifications by Name.* Retrieved August 23, 2009, from Microsoft website: http://www.microsoft.com/learning/en/us/certification/view-by-name.aspx.

Microsoft Corporation. n.d. *Training.* Retrieved June 24, 2008, from Microsoft Corporation website: www.microsoft.com/training.

Microsoft Developers Network. December 2007. *The Infrastructure Landscape: A Matter of Perspective.* Retrieved November 11, 2008, from Microsoft Corporation MSDN Architect Center website: http://msdn.microsoft.com/en-us/library/bb896739.aspx.

Microsoft Press. 1998. *Networking Essentials: MCSE Self-Paced Kit (Microsoft Training Product)*. Redmond, WA: Microsoft Press.

Norton, M. J. January 1, 2001. *Networking as a 2nd Language*. Retrieved from O'Reilly website: http://www.oreillynet.com/pub/ct/23.

Oracle Press. n.d. *Oracle® Database VLDB and Partitioning Guide*. Retrieved April 12, 2009, from Oracle Corporate website: http://download.oracle.com/docs/cd/B28359_01/server.111/b32024/part_admin.htm.

Patton, R. 2006. *Software Testing*. Indianapolis, IN: Sams Publishing.

Pendse, Nigel. n.d. *The OLAP Report*. Retrieved February 9, 2009, from Business Application Research Center website: http://www.olapreport.com/glossary.htm.

Platt, M. n.d. *Architecture Type Definitions*. Retrieved November 12, 2008, from Michael Platt Weblog: Blogs.technet.com/michael_platt/archive/2005/10/07/412167.aspx.

Procedural programming. August 13, 2009. *Wikipedia, The Free Encyclopedia*. Retrieved August 13, 2009, from http://en.wikipedia.org/w/index.php?title=Procedural_programming&oldid=307715937.

Project Management Institute (PMI). n.d. *About PMI's Credentials*. Retrieved October 1, 2009, from PMI website: http://www.pmi.org/CareerDevelopment/Pages/AboutPMIsCredentials.aspx.

Quality Assurance Institute. n.d. *Software Testing Certification*. Retrieved October 1, 2009, from QAI Global Institute website: http://www.qaiglobalinstitute.com/innerpages/Default.asp.

Red Hat. n.d. *Red Hat Certification*. Retrieved January 29, 2009, from Red Hat website: http://www.redhat.com/training/.

Rozanski, N., and E. Woods. 2005. *Software Systems Architecture: Working with Stakeholders Using Viewpoints and Perspectives*. Upper Saddle River, NJ: Pearson Education.

Software Certifications Inc. n.d. *Certified Software Business Analyst (CSBA)*. Retrieved October 1, 2009, from Software Certifications website: http://www.softwarecertifications.org/qai_csba.htm.

Software Engineering Institute. 2015. *Structuring the Chief Information Security Officer Organization*. Retrieved October 15, 2017, from SEI website: https://insights.sei.cmu.edu/sei_blog/2016/02/structuring-the-chief-information-security-officer-ciso-organization.html/.

Sommerville, I. A. 1997. "Viewpoints: Principles, problems and a practical approach to requirements engineering." *Annals of Software Engineering* 3: 101–130.

Steinke, S. 2000. *Network Tutorial: A Complete Introduction to Networks.* San Francisco: CMP Books.

Sun Microsystems. n.d. *Java Certification.* Retrieved September 30, 2009, from Sun Microsystems website: http://www.sun.com/training/certification/java/index.xml.

University of Albany. n.d. *Glossary.* Retrieved August 10, 2008, from University of Albany website: www.albany.edu/its/glossary.htm.

University of California, Irvine. n.d. *Enterprise Architect Role.* Retrieved from University of California website: http://apps.adcom.uci.edu/EnterpriseArch/EARole.html.

VPN Tools. n.d. Networking Tools. Retrieved January 29, 2009 from www.vpntools.com.

Wang, W. 2008. *Beginning Programming for Dummies.* Indianapolis, IN: Wiley Publishing, Inc.

Wiegers, K. 1999. *Software Requirements.* Redmond, WA: Microsoft Press.

Wikipedia. n.d. Networking—LAN, WAN, Retrieved August 19, 2009, from www.wikipedia.org.

Wreski, D. August 22, 1998. *Linux Security Administrator's Guide v0.98.* Retrieved September 10, 2009, from http://www.nic.com/~dave/SecurityAdminGuide/SecurityAdminGuide.html.

References

Apache. 2018. "Apache™ Hadoop®!" Retrieved March 13, 2018, from http://hadoop.apache.org/.

Bishop, M. 2007. *Introduction to Computer Security.* Addison-Wesley Professional.

CNBC. 2018. "Amazon lost cloud market share to Microsoft in the fourth quarter: KeyBanc." Retrieved March 14, 2018, from https://www.cnbc.com/2018/01/12/

amazon-lost-cloud-market-share-to-microsoft-in-the-fourth-quarter-keybanc.html.

Davenport, T., and Patil, D. 2012. "Data Scientist: The Sexiest Job of the 21ˢᵗ Century." Retrieved March 13, 2018, from https://hbr.org/2012/10/data-scientist-the-sexiest-job-of-the-21ˢᵗ-century.

Gartner. 2017. "2017 IT Budget." *Gartner.* Retrieved from http://www.gartner.com/explore/tools/itbudget.

https://www.owasp.org/index.php XSS_(Cross_Site_Scripting)_Prevention_Cheat Sheet.

IBM. (2014). The big deal about big data. 2014 Smarter Business Summit.

Longbing, C. 2017. "Data science: a comprehensive overview." *ACM Computing Surveys* 50 (3), 42.

Mell, P., and Grance, T. 2011. The NIST definition of cloud computing.

Microsoft. 2017. "Securing the cloud—Microsoft Story Labs." Retrieved March 14, 2018, from https://news.microsoft.com/stories/cloud-security/.

Naur, P. 1968. "'Datalogy,' the science of data and data processes." *IFIP Congress, 2,* 1383–1387.

NIST. 2014. "Cybersecurity Framework." Retrieved March 17, 2018, from https://www.nist.gov/cyberframework.

PearsonVue. 2016. "Value of IT Certification Survey." Retrieved March 15, 2018, from https://home.pearsonvue.com/Documents/Marketing/2016-Pearson-VUE-Value-of-IT-Certification-Survey_.aspx.

PRNewswire. 2017. "2017 Cloud Data Breaches Highlight Need for Ongoing Attention to Configuration and Management." Retrieved March 14, 2018, from https://www.prnewswire.com/news-releases/2017-cloud-data-breaches-highlight-need-for-ongoing-attention-to-configuration-and-management-300564664.html.

TekSystems. 2018. "The Value of IT Certifications." Retrieved March 15, 2018, from https://www.teksystems.com/en/resources/news-press/2016/the-value-of-it-certifications.

TheAtlantic. 2014. "The Details About the CIA's Deal with Amazon." *The Atlantic.* Retrieved March 14, 2018, from https://www.theatlantic.com/technology/archive/2014/07/the-details-about-the-cias-deal-with-amazon/374632/.

Sharda, R., Delen, D., & Turban, E. (2013). Business intelligence: A managerial perspective on analytics. Prentice-Hall.

White, T. (2012). Hadoop: The definitive guide. O'Reilly Media.

GLOSSARY

active directory (AD)
The directory service stores information about objects on a network and makes this information available to users and network administrators. Active directory gives network users access to permitted resources anywhere on the network using a single log-on process.

address resolution protocol (ARP)
Address resolution protocol maps hardware address to IP address for delivery of data on a local area network.

AppleTalk
A local area network protocol developed by Apple Computer.

asynchronous transfer mode (ATM)
Asynchronous transfer mode is a technology that can provide high-speed data transmission over LANs or WANs.

border gateway protocol version 4 (BGPv4)
Border gateway protocol allows routers to connect to each other.

configuration management
This is a process of tracking different development builds/versions of the software for revision, change, and release control.

domain

A domain is a group of computers that are part of a network and share a common directory database. A domain is administered as a unit with common rules and procedures.

domain name system (DNS)

DNS is a database system that translates an IP address into a hostname that is easy to remember. For example, converting an IP like 209.121.191.98 to kensington.com.

dynamic host configuration protocol (DHCP)

DHCP is a TCP/IP service protocol that dynamically leases IP addresses to eligible network client computers.

frame relay

Frame relay is a network technology used for connecting devices on the internet.

FreeBSD

FreeBSD is a flavor of UNIX operating system; it's free and originally from Berkeley Software Distribution (BSD).

generic route encapsulation (GRE)

Generic route encapsulation is a method of encapsulating any network protocol in another protocol.

Health Information Trust Alliance (HITRUST)

Health Information Trust Alliance is an organization that works within the health IT field to create what is known as the common security framework. This framework helps healthcare organizations secure sensitive health information.

Health Insurance Portability and Accountability Act (HIPAA)

Health insurance portability and accountability act is a legislation that was passed in 1996 that sets guidelines and rules for the protection and safeguarding of medical information.

Hot Standby Router Protocol (HSRP)

Hot Standby Router Protocol is a Cisco routing protocol for fault-tolerant IP routing that enables a set of routers to work together.

hypertext transfer protocol (HTTP/HTTPS)

In the OSI model, the hypertext transfer protocol is located in the application layer and is used for linking files, text, graphics, and so on between browsers and other applications on the internet.

integrated services digital network (ISDN)

Integrated services digital network is a wide area network data communication service provided by telephone companies. Used for high-speed dial-up connections to the internet for the delivery of data, audio, and video.

Internet Information Server (IIS)

IIS is a software service that supports website creation, configuration, and management, along with other internet functions.

internet message access protocol (IMAP)

Internet message access protocol is an internet protocol used for email retrieval.

internet protocol security (IPSec)

Internet protocol security is a protocol that secures IP communications with encryption, data authentication, and confidentiality.

internet protocol version 6 (IPv6)

IPv6 is a newer internet protocol version that expands the address length of 32 bits up to 128 bits.

Internetwork Packet Exchange / Sequenced Packet Exchange (IPX/SPX)

Internetwork Packet Exchange/Sequenced Packet Exchange is a network protocol used by Novell Netware.

lightweight directory access protocol (LDAP)
LDAP is a protocol for querying and accessing information directories—such as organizations, individuals, phone numbers, and addresses—and other resources, such as files and devices in a network.

listserv
Listserv is an electronic mailing list software used by people to communicate with other members that are subscribed to the list.

local area network (LAN)
A local area network is a computer network covering a small geographic area, like a home, or one location, such as an office or school.

MhonArc
Based on Perl programming language, MhonArc is a free email archiving program that converts mails to HTML.

National Institute of Standards and Technology (NIST)
National Institute of Standards and Technology is an agency of the US Department of Commerce with a charge to develop standards, frameworks, and measurements that promote innovations.

network file system (NFS)
This is a UNIX-based protocol that allows computers access to files over a network.

Network Information Systems and Yellow Pages (NIS/YP)
NIS/YP is used in the UNIX environment and operates similar to Windows DHCP, allowing computers within a domain to share common network addressing configurations.

open shortest path first (OSPF)
Open shortest path first is a routing protocol that determines the best path for routing IP traffic.

payment card industry data security (PCI-DS)
Payment card industry data security is an information security standard for organizations that accept, store, and transmit credit card information. These organizations must implement the standards to be in compliance.

point-to-point protocol (PPP)
Point-to-point protocol provides dial-up networked connection to networks. PPP is commonly used by internet service providers (ISPs) as the dial-up protocol for connecting customers to their networks.

post office protocol version 3 (POP3)
Located in the application layer of the OSI model, POP3 is an internet protocol used for delivering or receiving emails.

Postfix
Postfix is a free mail system that works on UNIX systems for the delivery and retrieval of emails.

Pretty Good Privacy (PGP)
PGP is a public key encryption system used for email communications.

procmail
Procmail is used in the UNIX environment as a mail delivery agent (MDA).

QMail
QMail is a mail component used on UNIX systems.

routing information protocol (RIP/RIP2)
Routing information protocol finds a route with the smallest number of hops between the source and destination.

Sarbanes–Oxley (SOX) Act
Sarbanes–Oxley Act is a law that was passed in 2002 that requires top management personnel in public companies to certify the accuracy of their financial information or be held accountable. This law was passed

to protect shareholders from fraudulent accounting practices. IT creates information security controls to ensure that financial data is secure and protected from loss.

secure shell (SSH)
SSH is a network protocol used for authenticating communications when logging onto a remote computer.

Sendmail
Similar to Postfix, Sendmail is a message transfer agent (MTA) used for the delivery and retrieval of emails.

simple mail transfer protocol (SMTP)
Simple mail transfer protocol is a TCP/IP protocol used in the process of sending and receiving emails.

simple network management protocol (SNMP)
Simple network management protocol allows network administrators to connect to and manage network devices.

Source Code Control (CVS, RCS, SCCS)
CVS—Concurrent Version System—is a free source control application that developers use to manage the versioning of their code. Same as RCS (Revision Control System) and SCCS (Source Code Control System).

Switched Multimegabit Data Service (SMDS)
Switched Multimegabit Data Service is a WAN with speeds of 1.544 to 45Mbps.

synchronous optical network (SONET)
Synchronous optical network identifies how fiber-optic technology can deliver voice, data, and video over network speeds over 1Gbps.

telnet
Telnet is an internet protocol that allows users to connect their PCs as remote workstations to a host computer anywhere in the world and

use that computer as if it were local. Telnet allows terminal emulation, which is the ability to access a remote computer and use its resources.

transmission control protocol / internet protocol (TCP/IP)
Transmission control protocol / internet protocol is used in the interconnection of computers on the internet.

user acceptance test (UAT)
Also known as end-user testing, this is the type of testing performed by customers on a production system to approve, accept, and sign off on a project.

user datagram protocol (UDP)
User datagram protocol provides a connectionless transportation service on top of the internet protocol (IP).

virtual private network (VPN)
The extension of a private network, including encapsulated, encrypted, and authenticated links across shared or public networks.

wide area network (WAN)
A wide area network is a data communications network that is geographically separated. WAN computer networks usually span several locations.

X Windows System
X Windows is a software program used in the UNIX environment that provides a graphical user interface (GUI) much like a Windows system.

INDEX

S

SaaS 243
Scripting language 126
SDET 166
server 53
Server Based Networks 54
Silverlight 26
Simple Mail Transfer Protocol
    (SMTP) 79
software bugs 149
Software development life cycle
    (SDLC) 96
software testing 149
solution architect 90
SQL Profiler 191
sql reporting analyst 172
SQL Server Reporting Services
    (SSRS) 103
Sqoop 203
Static IP address 65
Storage Architect 90
Stored Procedures 171
Structured Query Language 171
Sun Solaris 74

T

table 171
technical project manager 118
Telnet 81
test plan 154
threa 219
total cost of ownership (TCO) 93
T-SQL (Transact–SQL) 103

U

UML 175

V

version control 29
Views 171

Virtual Private Network (VPN) 61
visualization 204
Visual Studio .Net 25
vulnerability 219

W

White Box Testing 155
Wide Area Networks (WAN) 60
Windows Presentation Foundation 142

Z

z/OS mainframe operating system 77

Printed in the United States
By Bookmasters